The Good American

The Good American

A Situation Report for Citizens

B. Sidney Smith

The Institute for Economic Democracy

Institute for Economic Democracy
PO Box 309, Appomattox VA 24522, USA.

Smith, Becker Sidney. *The Good American: A Situation Report for Citizens.*
ISBN: 978-1-933567-43-3

Contents

Introduction

This book was written as Americans were held captive by a presidential campaign season. For the Democrats we had incumbent Barack Obama, who campaigned in 2008 on themes of Hope and Change and as the antidote to eight years of George W. Bush's policies of tax-cuts for the rich at home and bombs for Muslims abroad, policies that all good liberals loudly professed (at the time) to find intolerable. This time around he appeared to run on the theme of not being a Republican, as the rich still had their tax-cuts and the Muslims still received their bombs, many now delivered by remote control.

For the Republicans we had Mitt Romney, the former governor of Massachusetts and poster boy of the financial elite, who labored at the unenviable task of running against policy positions that were largely his own not so many years before. To aid him in this effort he selected congressman Paul Ryan of Wisconsin, an anti-government true-believer whose career has been dedicated to dismantling the few remaining defenses, such as Medicare and Social Security, that working Americans have against utter thralldom to the owners.

Billions were invested by the wealthiest 0.01% of Americans in what has not for generations been a war of ideas but a war of rival advertising campaigns, of national brands competing to sell to bewildered political consumers what amounts to the same product. To the winners go the spoils. It makes aging fans of The Firesign Theatre like me wistful for the days of George Papoon and his running mate George Leroy Tirebiter, the perennial nominees of the Natural Surrealist Light People's Party, who campaigned on the slogan, "Not Insane." That at least made sense.

Thank Heaven for the independent parties. The Green Party USA nominated Dr. Jill Stein, a woman of compassion, intelligence, and integrity, the Libertarian Party nominated Governor Gary Johnson, the Constitution Party put forward Congressman

Virgil Goode, and the Justice Party had Mayor Rocky Anderson. Each of these candidates and several others offered policies to deliver real economic and political reform characterized by common sense—and by principles of government that are deeply rooted in the American tradition. Voters who prefer Jeffersonian democracy to the present oligarchy were at least able to mark their ballot with civic pride and a clear conscience. More than 2 million did so.

It is the failure of the present establishment—including the media establishment—to address the actual crises we face that motivated the writing of this book. The times are not just a-changin' any more; the elements of American life have begun to swirl like dry leaves before a coming storm.

The country has been riven by crises before, it will be noted, and if the past were a sure guide we could be confident that the republic will survive and long endure, as the saying goes. Is there really anything on the horizon to rival such previous cataclysms as our civil war, the Great Depression, or the waves of social unrest and political violence that swept the country in the past?

Regrettably, yes. The present threats to our economy, our civic commons and democratic institutions, our environment, our security, and our liberty are simultaneous and severe, and in numerous respects unprecedented in our history.

In these pages I offer a plain-spoken report to my fellow citizens on the state of affairs confronting us, together with a call to civic duty. We own these problems, but we do not yet own the solutions. Let us labor now together in solidarity, that we may leave for coming generations of Americans a country and a world in which justice reigns, liberty is secured, and the existential threats we now face are consigned to the pages of history.

B. Sidney Smith
Appomattox, Virginia
Sep 2012 (updated Feb 2013)

for Jill and Cheri

1 A Tale of Two Countries

This is really a book about two nations, not one. In some ways, it is about two nations that could scarcely be more different, although each might be considered the nation with the greatest impact on world affairs—in much of the past as well as the present.

The first nation has been, throughout its history, much admired around the world. It was conceived during the Age of Enlightenment, a time when western civilization was at last shrugging off the idea that rulers got to rule because God said so. The founders of this country declared openly and radically that the rights and powers of government come not from the divine will but from the consent of the governed.[1] In the preamble to its constitution the purposes of such a just government are made plain: to establish justice, to insure domestic tranquility, to provide for the common defense, to promote the general welfare, and to secure the blessings of liberty to its citizens.

Despite many challenges and unforeseen problems, this nation remains dedicated to the founding documents in which these principles are articulated. Dozens of other nations, when instituting their own democratic traditions, took this nation as their model. But this nation has done much more than merely to articulate admirable principles. It has opened its arms to more than 65 million of the world's oppressed and dispossessed,[2] providing a new homeland to more than a fifth of the entire world's present immigrant population.[3] It has led the world in promoting the democratic principle of government, including the extension of the right to participate in governance to all adult persons without prejudice. It has been on the front line of some of history's most pivotal bat-

1

tles against tyranny, spending its treasury and its blood in defense
of liberty and fundamental human rights.

This nation of which I speak is one of which I am deeply proud
to be a citizen, for it is the United States.

The second nation I ask you to consider is undoubtedly the
most violent nation in the history of humankind. Born in war, it
has engaged in one or more military actions, interventions, or clandestine operations beyond its own borders in nearly every year of
its existence.[4][5] At least sixteen of these military adventures had
the express aim, generally successful, of wresting territory from
other nations, and as many more were efforts to topple the governments of other countries, most of them democratically elected.
In addition to foreign aggressions it has undertaken 14 major wars
and hundreds of smaller actions against its own indigenous population, with the aim and effect of largely eliminating it.[6]

Although it has ratified the United Nations Convention on the
Prevention and Punishment of the Crime of Genocide, it was with
the proviso that it holds itself immune from prosecution for that
crime, unlike 132 other signatories,[7] and it opposes the International Criminal Court, a permanent tribunal to prosecute individuals for genocide, crimes against humanity, war crimes, and the
crime of aggression.[8] Indeed it exhibits a pattern of contempt for
international institutions that promote peace and justice. For example, it spurned the International Court of Justice when it was
convicted by that court in 1986 of illegal acts of aggression against
another country,[9] refusing to pay the fine and reparations imposed
despite a near-unanimous UN resolution urging it to do so.[10] It also
refuses to enter into international agreements, signed by almost
every other country, banning the use of weapons such as land-
mines[11] and cluster munitions[12] that maim and kill the innocent
for years after their deployment. These weapons, which it continues to manufacture and deploy, kill thousands of men, women, and
children every year.[13]

In addition to its own military forces this nation employs

tens of thousands of private military "contractors"[14][15]—really, mercenaries—accountable to no external oversight or system of justice.[16] These contractors are known to be responsible for many atrocities including murder and torture.[17] In the past private contractors on this nation's payroll are known to have committed acts of overt terrorism, including the bombing of a civilian airliner in flight, bombing of hotels, assassinations, and so on. It continues to harbor many of these terrorists on its own soil, refusing lawful extradition requests from other countries seeking to bring these criminals to justice.[18]

This nation leads the world in the research and stockpiling of weapons of mass destruction, including chemical, biological, and nuclear weapons.[19] It refuses to renounce the first-use of such weapons, or their use to enforce its will on other countries,[20] and it remains the only country in history to have demonstrated its willingness to use weapons of mass destruction on densely populated civilian targets to achieve its aims.[21] Recently it militarized the internet, creating powerful cyberweapons and using them in a covert aggressive war against another nation.[22]

This country reserves to itself alone the right to attack and destroy any country that threatens its interests, as it alone defines those interests, and it has publicly declared its intent to achieve military domination of the planet.[23]

These facts make it less surprising, if no less horrifying, that this nation is directly responsible for the deaths of at least 3 million non-combatant civilians in just the last 50 years. This is a conservative estimate.[24]

Incredibly, the majority of this nation's citizens are not cognizant of these facts. So effective is the propaganda in this country that according to respected, mainstream sociological studies those members of its society who regularly view the primary domestic sources of news and information actually know less about their country's role in the world than those who do not.[25]

This nation's record on human rights is no less troubling. Its economic divide is vast, with 80% of its population sharing less than 7% of its financial wealth, the rest reserved to a wealthy ruling class.[26] Owing to a draconian justice system that includes harsh mandatory sentencing even for non-violent offenses,[27] and perhaps also owing to the fact that its prison system is increasingly run for profit,[28] with only one-twentieth of the world's population it houses nearly one-fourth of its prisoners, more than 2 million, more than any other country.[29] Half a million of these are known to be mentally ill, often severely.[30] One hundred thousand of these prisoners are children. Nearly ten thousand are serving life sentences for crimes committed *while* they were children, something unimaginable in almost any other part of the world. Somalia is the only other country besides this one not to ratify the UN Convention on the Rights of the Child.[31]

The leaders of this country reserve to themselves alone the right to seize[32] or assassinate[33] citizens of any country (including their own), anywhere in the world, secretly, and to suspend any or all of their rights, including the right to challenge their confinement before an independent judiciary, the rights of petition and representation, the right of security from torture and other maltreatment or affronts to personal dignity, and any other right vouchsafed by the Geneva Conventions, international law, or the laws of any country.[34]

This is a nation disliked and distrusted by an overwhelming majority of the world's citizens, according to respected international polls,[35] a nation whose foreign policy most view as the primary cause of many of the present conflicts around the globe, and a grave danger—indeed the foremost danger—to the future security of the world's people.[36]

It is a nation for which, as a citizen, I am grief-stricken with shame. For this nation too is the United States.

2 The Great Infant

That the two nations described in the last chapter could be the same nation is hard to believe. That is, it is hard for Americans to believe. Elsewhere in the world it is commonly understood, especially in regions where people have fallen on the wrong side of our national self-interest. Americans, however, not only don't tend to believe it, they aren't usually mindful even of the existence of the second nation described, even as it dominates politics at home and geopolitics abroad. The question of how such insensitivity to our own role on the stage of nations could come about has been a consuming interest of mine and (fortunately) of many others better equipped by skill and training to answer such questions.

The answer reveals itself when we consider the mental life of the typical American, a mental life that has changed radically over the last few generations in a manner that was planned nearly a century ago. In brief, Americans have been subjected to a program of psychological denaturing meant to pacify them and to condition them to respond to mass manipulation of their tastes, prejudices, and attitudes. There is overwhelming evidence that this program has largely succeeded, that it is under the control of an integrated corporate and government elite, and that it has grave implications for our future.

A central and pioneering figure of this project was Edward Bernays, the founder of the field of public relations, also called propaganda. In *Propaganda* (1928), Bernays wrote:

> The conscious and intelligent manipulation of the or-
> ganized habits and opinions of the masses is an im-

> portant element in democratic society. Those who
> manipulate this unseen mechanism of society consti-
> tute an invisible government which is the true ruling
> power of our country. ...We are governed, our minds
> are molded, our tastes formed, our ideas suggested,
> largely by men we have never heard of. ...In almost
> every act of our daily lives, whether in the sphere of
> politics or business, in our social conduct or our ethi-
> cal thinking, we are dominated by the relatively small
> number of persons...who understand the mental pro-
> cesses and social patterns of the masses. It is they
> who pull the wires which control the public mind.[37]

The principles and techniques of manipulation that Bernays developed were from the beginning placed in the service of both public and private enterprises, as well as governments. His early successes included work on the Creel Commission established by Woodrow Wilson to convince Americans to enter World War I,[38] a campaign for the American Tobacco Company in 1929 to break the taboo against women smoking in public, and pro-grams on behalf of President Calvin Coolidge's reelection cam-paign, the American Dental Association, the NAACP, Proctor & Gamble, and many others.[39] His techniques drew heavily from the sciences of psychology and sociology and the writings of such psychoanalysts as Ivan Pavlov and Bernays' own un-cle, Sigmund Freud. These techniques proved wildly success-ful and were quickly adopted by propagandists around the world. Joseph Göbbels, the propaganda minister of Nazi Germany, drew on Bernays' writings when he instigated the Holocaust against Eu-ropean Jews.[40] In 1954 Bernays himself was hired by the United Fruit Company, working with the Eisenhower administration, to brand the democratically elected President Guzmán of Guatemala as a communist so that he could be deposed in a CIA-engineered coup.[41]

The use of "public relations" as a tool of mass manipulation was already commonplace in America by the middle of the 20th century,[42] but two events served to prioritize its importance in the minds of the ruling elites. First, the Great Depression of the 1930's revealed that the American working class, when faced with economic breakdown and material ruin, was capable of organizing itself into a formidable political force that could threaten the social and economic order.[43] One can only imagine the unease in American boardrooms under the shadow of socialist and nationalist overthrows of the old order in Europe as armies of angry Americans gathered spontaneously into political opposition groups of such ferocity as to make today's Occupy movement seem almost cute by comparison. World War II and the induction of 10 million men into uniform[44] bought them time, and by the end of the war the propaganda machinery was well placed to engineer the enduring communist scare of the 1950's and 60's that served to brand any organized resistance to government policy as un-American,[45] and served as well to justify a dramatically increased American military hegemony abroad.[46]

The second event to cement the primacy of propaganda in American culture was the need to maintain the artificially high levels of production and consumption achieved during the war to avoid another economic depression and a return to the social upheavals of the 1930's. In short, Americans had to be trained to purchase ever-increasing amounts of consumable goods:

> Our enormously productive economy demands that we make consumption our way of life, that we convert the buying and use of goods into rituals, that we seek our spiritual satisfaction and our ego satisfaction in consumption. We need things consumed, burned up, worn out, replaced and discarded at an ever-increasing rate.[47]

Americans were not well-suited to consumerism. The heirs of a pioneer culture and survivors of both war and hard times, working Americans in the first half of the 20th century valued self-reliance, thrift, and conservation.[48][49] They mended clothing and repaired tools and appliances rather than replacing them. They grew much of their own food, prepared it themselves, and preserved it too. Although consumer culture, spread through the mediums of print, radio, and movies in the 1920's and 30's, had already begun to transform American life,[50] it was after World War II that Americans were at last persuaded *en masse* to embrace the ethos of consumption.[51] Although there were many reasons for this, the influence of one new technology was decisive.

From the time television became a universal fixture in American households in the 1950's it has been the primary tool for commercial, social, and political propaganda.[52] Currently, between television, the internet, and mobile/broadband, a typical American watches 4 to 6 hours per day (depending on age) of commercial video entertainment.[53] As measured by household viewing hours, Americans watch more than twice as much television as people in other developed countries.[54] More than a third of this time is spent watching advertisements,[55] not counting in-show product placements and promotion. However, much more—typically more than five times more—is invested in the commercials (in the aggregate) than in the programming for a typical hour of television.[56] Ad agencies hire top writers, directors, and production talent, with the result that the commercials have higher "production values" than the regular programming used to lure viewers attention to them. They also use sophisticated research methods to pinpoint consumers' vulnerabilities, and hire experts in psychological manipulation to enhance the effectiveness of their ads.[57][58][59] Total annual spending on public relations in the United States tops $1 trillion.[60] More than $100 billion is spent on television and internet advertising each year.[61]

In short, most Americans' day is punctuated by a quick and

steady drumbeat of messages whose purpose is to create wants that can only be gratified through consumption (in the case of product ads) or by the adoption of an externally validated opinion, attitude, or identity (in the case of more general propaganda); messages moreover crafted by experts specifically to induce the viewer, listener, or reader to suspend their critical faculties and yield to a childish impulse.

The "payload" of these messages—the product or opinion being foisted on the consumer—is ultimately under the control of the media company. In the last thirty years the diversity of ownership in media that once characterized the industry has vanished; through mergers and vertical integration just six companies, themselves in many cases deeply interconnected, control nearly every commercial source of print, broadcast, cinema, and internet entertainment and information.[62] These corporations are not only interconnected with each other but with other major industries, including defense (weapons manufacturers), energy (big oil and coal), finance (major banks and insurers), pharmaceuticals, and agribusiness.[63]

It is not just what Americans see, hear, and read that is under elite control, it is what they don't see, don't hear, and don't read. They see no substantive information about the corporations that own the media or that are interconnected with the media—in effect, the influence and activities of elite power are air-brushed out of the picture.[64][65] Foreign reporting by American journalists has all but vanished with the shuttering of foreign news bureaus by media conglomerates, so Americans see little and know less about the world beyond their borders where 95% of human beings live.[66][67][68] At the same time national and local news reporting is dominated by personality and lifestyle-oriented "infotainment"[69][70] so Americans aren't shown the wrecked communities and grinding poverty that consumerism and unregulated exploitation have strewn across their own landscape,[71] nor are they exposed to voices or ideas that challenge the assumptions and agendas of those with power.[72] Government institutions, especially the executive branch and the military, manipulate media coverage of their policies and activities, ensuring that only those writers and broadcasters committed to presenting them in a positive light are given full access, while those who are critical or who challenge official accounts are marginalized, silenced, or sometimes even prosecuted.[73] [74]

The material world in which Americans live is nearly as synthetic as the one they see on their screens. Americans do not know how their appliances, automobiles, or electronics function, and have little choice but to replace them at frequent intervals.[75] They have at best a vague notion of how or where the energy they use to heat and cool their homes and offices, to operate their appliances, or to run their automobiles is produced and distributed, or the consequences for both the environment and their government's foreign and domestic policy. They do not know what their garments are made of, or who by, or where. They do not know what is in their food, how it is produced, or how or by whom it is prepared.[76] My own research with college students over the years suggests that at most 1 in 6 Americans knows how to cook a balanced and nutritious meal starting with fresh ingredients. Utterly lacking in self-sufficiency, most Americans' lives are—literally and absolutely—dependent on the uninterrupted operation of the consumer economy.

Americans view education at all levels as a means to an end rather than an end in itself.[77] Young Americans in particular have no sense of purpose that is not framed by their place in the consumer economy. They indebt themselves to go to school to obtain a degree, which they view not as a certificate of merit but as a license to sell their labor for a higher price, to have increased spending power and socio-economic status. This is called "playing by the rules."[78] Most achieve their highest educational degree (high school diploma or bachelor's degree) without mastering basic mathematical skills,[79] without a working knowledge of science or scientific principles,[80] without the capacity to read or write at what used to be considered a college level,[81] without meaningful exposure to the cultural heritage of western civilization,[82 83 84 85] and without a clear grasp of civics or the machinery of government.[86 87] Most Americans know far more about what is fashionable to wear, current sports statistics, the television entertainment schedule, the newest generation of electronic gadgetry, and the life-events of celebrities they will never meet than they do about any of the government policies or public or private institutions that actually affect their lives.

Another result of the enclosure of the American mind by commercial and governmental propaganda is that Americans have come to exhibit a set of attitudes very different from those of people in other countries on a range of issues—even people in the countries culturally and economically most similar to ours. Americans are far more concerned with personal gratification and far less with the well-being of others, dismiss the importance of factors over which they have no control, favor unilateral and militaristic solutions to world problems over international cooperation, are more isolationist when they are not interventionist, and are more likely to believe themselves culturally superior.[88] Americans are also more likely to believe in the possibility of their personally joining the ranks of the rich and powerful, even though this is actually harder to do in the United States than in other free societies.[89] The widespread belief among Americans in American exceptionalism is particularly striking in light of the fact that America has fallen behind other developed countries on every measure of cultural progress and social well-being, in many respects far, far behind.[90] Americans don't live in the real America, but in a virtual America conjured into their heads by a lifetime of mental and emotional conditioning.

The aim of the propagandists was two-fold. First, Americans were to adopt a narrative about themselves and their country that is so exalting that it correlates approval of the United States with moral rectitude, equates consumerism with personal freedom, and colors all criticism of the nation or its economic system as disloyal, extreme, and destructive. At the same time, Americans were to be lulled into apathy towards the conduct of government[91] and sufficiently distracted from it as to be at little risk of critically assessing its policies or operations.[92] Second, Americans had to commit to personal consumption as the means and the measure of their quality of life.

These aims have been achieved, but at this cost: Americans on the whole are childish in their tastes, opinions, and discourse, they have lost their critical and imaginative faculties, and they are as disinclined to govern themselves as they are unfit.

3 Land of Elites

The typical American described in Chapter 2 is not every American. Some Americans are properly educated, some are self-reliant, and some have even emancipated themselves from consumerism. But very few even of these Americans have significant influence on the country or the lives of people in it. The number of Americans with real influence is very small, and their influence is very, very great. Although they are not organized into a formal institution, they nonetheless constitute the "invisible government" Edward Bernays wrote about in 1928.

It is enough to follow the money. From its earliest years the United States has been a land of the wealthy few and the marginalized many. Long before industrialization, in the large population centers of the east coast, the richest few percent controlled 80% or more of the wealth, while by 1910 (the earliest available data for income) the top 10% of American households had a larger income than the bottom 50%.[93] Another way to put it is that for every dollar earned by labor, the owners claimed more than five dollars.

After the last Great Depression and following World War II, the country experienced thirty years of somewhat lessened inequality. Programs such as Social Security, a high rate of taxation on corporate income, and a progressive schedule of personal income tax rates helped to empower working people to claim a larger proportion of income. Together with increased productivity owing to improved technology and management, working Americans' larger incomes fueled a long period of stable economic expansion. However, from approximately 1980 to the present the gains of increased productivity have gone almost entirely to the wealthiest 1% of Americans, while income distribution and tax rates have returned to historical norms in what has been called the Great Divergence.[94]

Just as happened many times in the past, most dramatically in the crash of 1929, this inequality led to a breakdown of the financial system in 2008, and here in the 2010s we are living through a Great Depression that closely parallels that of the 1930s, characterized again by extreme disparities between wealth and poverty and the material ruin of the middle class. Income disparity in the United States is now markedly greater than in any other western democracy, worse even than in many undeveloped, autocratic regimes.[95]

By the numbers: Half of American households are either "low-income" or in poverty.[96] At the other end of the scale, the richest 1% takes 24% of the income.[97] The 400 richest Americans have more wealth than the bottom 150 million.[98] Measured just in terms of financial wealth, the top 1% has nearly 43% of the wealth and the next 19% controls another 50%, leaving just 7% of the total financial wealth of the country in the hands of the bottom 80% of Americans. The top 1% controls 62% of the business equity and 61% of the securities, while the bottom 90% controls only 7% and 2% respectively.[99] In 1980 the top executives in corporations were paid 42 times the average worker's pay; by 2011 they were being paid 380 times the average worker's pay. Since the current economic collapse began the incomes of the top 1% have risen 11.6% while average incomes (for those who can find employment) in the bottom 99% remain essentially unchanged.[100][101] Using the methodology the government used until 1994 unemployment hovers, at the time of this writing, at 15–16%.[102] If the long-term (>1 year) unemployed are counted, the rate is probably around 22%.[103]

Those are Great Depression numbers, but it does not tell the whole story. The principal asset for most Americans is their home, if they own one, but in the 2008 crash 55% of homeowner equity was lost, more than $7.3 trillion.[104] An additional $3.4 trillion evaporated from retirement accounts such as 401(k)s and IRAs.[105] That money is never coming back, not during the lifetimes of those who lost it. The American middle class, carefully cultivated in the generation following World War II, has been wiped out. The wealth they built is gone, and the infrastructure and jobs needed to rebuild it are gone. The owners are doing fine.

The only institution capable of redressing these imbalances will not do so. Because of the propaganda successes outlined previously a majority of Americans are convinced that government is the cause of their problems and should be prevented from enacting policies meant to help them.[106] Moreover, no politician at the state or national level can receive the enormous contributions necessary to compete in political campaigns except by promising to serve the owners' interests. As of the 8th of August, 2.5 million people had donated up to $200 each to the 2012 campaigns, but this amounts to only 18% of the funds raised. The top 2,100 donors had given $200 million—with 3 months of campaigning yet to go—and this does not include the much greater amounts given by billionaires, in secret, to bogus non-profits and so-called superPACs to support their candidates. The owners own the politicians too.[107]

Not content merely to keep elected leaders dependent on their patronage, financial elites also shape and often actually write the laws. When the politicians they own are in office, the representatives of elite interests are employed on the public payroll as their legislative directors and assistants. When out of office, the same individuals are employed as lobbyists.[108 109] In either capacity their role is the same: to write or edit the legislation that is passed by the House of Representatives and the Senate to insure that it reflects the will of the interests they represent.[110 111] This practice is also commonplace in state legislatures, even as it is organized at the national level.[112]

The things our national, state, and local governments are directed to do on behalf of elite interests make a long list. Topping the list is a tax code that allows the wealthiest to pay modest taxes on their income, and frequently allows them to avoid paying taxes altogether.[113] The wealthiest Americans keep the bulk of their wealth, $7–$10 trillion, in secret overseas tax havens beyond the view or reach of the IRS.[114][115] Corporations, in collusion with legislatures, have devised schemes that permit them to treat income as expenses by, for example, deducting profits transferred directly to executives through stock options, accelerating depreciations on investments, deferring taxes to future years, and setting up subsidiaries of themselves in tax-free countries like the Cayman Islands and then "paying" their profits to the subsidiaries. As a result, twenty-six of the largest companies, including AT&T, Boeing, and Citigroup, paid more to their own C.E.O.s than they did in taxes in 2011.[116] Coporate taxes as a percentage of all federal revenues have fallen from over 27% in 1955 to less than 9% today. During the same period, payroll taxes paid by working people increased from 58% to more than 81% of federal revenues.[117]

Direct cash subsidies from the federal government to energy, agriculture, pharmaceutical, and other large corporations amount to $100 billion every year.[118][119] This does not include frequent government bailouts of financial institutions to cover the losses incurred by banks and insurers. From 1980 to 1999 the loss to taxpayers at the national level for covering bad mortgage loans was $124 billion.[120] This figure does not include additional bailouts by states and municipalities during that period. While such bailouts have been common in the past, they are dwarfed by the enormous transfer of money from the public to private lenders following the 2008 crash. Between 2008 and 2012 taxpayers have lost $169 billion to bailout the major mortgage companies.[121] The Troubled Asset Relief Program (TARP—created to buy junk assets from investment banks) will ultimately cost taxpayers more than $47 billion, and the bailout of the major automakers such as General Motors and Chrysler will cost $25 billion.[122] During the same period the Federal Reserve has loaned at least $3 *trillion* to banks at near-zero interest, which the banks have frequently used to purchase treasury bonds that yield a comparatively much higher rate of interest—in effect loaning the money *back* to the government and earning free profit from the taxpayers.[123]

The "costs to taxpayers" listed in the previous paragraph are government estimates based on the assumption that the economy fully recovers and the financial recipients of the bailouts pay back everything they are supposed to. But in fact the government disbursed $13 trillion to America's top banks and corporations in the year following the crash.[124] This is more than 16 times the size of the "stimulus package" that was passed to help non-elite Americans weather the economic crisis—actually it was 26 times bigger if you only count the part of the stimulus that was real spending, not tax breaks.[125]

Many volumes could be filled with examples of government being induced to transfer the wealth of the people to private hands, from the giveaways of the nation's mining[126] and grazing[127] rights and its broadcast spectrum[128] to targeted tax breaks to favor specific interests.[129] But all of this corporate welfare—the bailouts, the tax breaks, all of it—is dwarfed by the grand giveaway that President Eisenhower named "The Military Industrial Complex."[130]

The Cold War ended more than 20 years ago and the United States has not been under threat of attack by any rival military since that time. Yet our government spends 20% of it's budget on the Defense Department alone, more than $700 billion,[131] higher than at any time since World War II.[132] Considering just federal funds (so not including Social Security, which is self-funding), and adding in the military portions of other federal departments' budgets, the cost of past military operations (including veteran's benefits and the interest on debt incurred for military expenditures), and the budget for intelligence operations, the total yearly federal outlay for the MIC at more than $1.2 trillion is well over half of the entire federal budget.[133] The United States military budget dwarfs that of its allies, and its allies and the United States taken together spend many times more than the entire rest of the world, including Russia and China, combined.[134] Alone the United States outspends China by a factor of 4 to 1, and every other country in the world by at least 10 to 1.[135] In *addition* to regular military spending, the final costs of the Iraq and Afghanistan wars is expected to be $4 trillion.[136]

These vast expenses only make sense, not from a need for increased national security, but as a means of transferring the wealth of the nation. The bulk of the funds expended go to private profit; the biggest chunk of all to arms manufacturers. The United States produces 60% of the world's armaments. Much is sold abroad, but most is purchased by our government.[137] Thirteen of the twenty largest arms manufacturers are American companies,[138] and they spend more than $17 million annually on lobbyists.[139] But war brings profits to many favored industries, from the financial sector to energy, general manufacturing, construction, and special services.[140]

Government in the United States is of, by, and for its most elite citizens. The national and state legislatures and the executive administrations of the country operate day to day on behalf of private rather than public interest, in a system that in any other context would be immediately recognized as one of organized criminality.

So what about the judicial branch? Although the nation's founders believed that governance should be reserved to the elites, they were adamant that all should be equal before the law. John Adams' famous phrase that the United States must be a "government of laws, not men"[141] has always in principle (if not always in practice) been a core value of our nation.

In his ground-breaking book *With Liberty and Justice for Some: How the Law Is Used to Destroy Equality and Protect the Powerful*, Glenn Greenwald exhaustively documents the ways in which the nation's elites have come to enjoy immunity from legal consequences for even the most serious law-breaking. The justice system has always been two-tiered, in the sense that a defendant has always been entitled to the best defense he or she can afford, but in the last 25 years a new ethos has been established that exempts our most elite citizens from having to concern themselves with the justice system at all.

In America today ordinary citizens face harsh punishments even for crimes that are minor or victimless. Meanwhile, serious crimes committed by elites are not even investigated—even when the crimes are publicly boasted about by the perpetrators. Widely known instances include lying to Congress, destruction of official records to cover up law-breaking, illegally spying on Americans by secretly intercepting their electronic communications, kidnapping, unlawful detention, and torture. The deliberate lies that took the nation to war in Iraq have been excused. The massive and deliberate fraud of ordinary investors and home-buyers that brought about the worst economic crisis in 70 years—not to be investigated or punished. The multiple war crimes that are still being committed abroad, the violations of international treaties and conventions, and the extraordinary malfeasance that have been committed in the "War on Terror" are just not the legal system's concern. In the major media the fact that these crimes go not just unpunished but uninvestigated is met with editorial approval, explicitly on the grounds that the most elite members of society should be shielded from the legal consequences, even for serious crimes, that non-elite Americans face for any infraction.[142]

Elites are not defined by how much power and money they have, but by how much more of these things they have than everybody else. The vast majority of Americans face a harsh truth: the wealth of their nation that they themselves built has been plundered, their government has turned on them, and their lives are poor, powerless, and without prospects.

4 All the Bunnies in the Meadow Die

Take a pinch of the spores of a certain fungus and drop them into a gallon jug, one whose walls are coated with nutrient so the fungus can grow as fast as it likes. Suppose you do this one morning, and that exactly 4 days later you find that the fungus has filled the jar and is just beginning to overflow it. How full was the jug the morning of the 3rd day?

    A. Three-quarters full.

    B. Half full.

    C. One-quarter full.

    D. Mostly empty.

This question is one I pose to students in general math courses at the start of my standard lecture on modeling natural growth, a lecture with the deliberately provocative title of this chapter. I find that if the lecture isn't provocative students are unlikely to absorb the main point, because people tend to think of growth as something steady. Trees grow a few feet each year just as children grow by 5 to 7 pounds each year. Our lives grow with the steady accumulation of the years themselves.

Growth, we think, means adding a fixed amount for each fixed period of time. But most natural growth is nothing like that. In most kinds of natural growth it is not a fixed amount but a *proportional* amount that is added at regular intervals. This is why so many rates of growth, such as the growth of an investment or the growth of a population, are expressed in *percentages-per-unit-time*.

If natural growth matched our intuition, the jug would be three-fourths full the day before it overflows. But in fact the jug is still mostly empty the day before. The correct answer is D. One way of understanding how this could be so is to think in terms of doubling times. In natural growth the time it takes for whatever is growing to double in size is always the same regardless of how big or small it is. For the fungus to fill a gallon jug in 4 days starting from just a pinch means it has to double about once very 7 hours or so.[143] So 7 hours before the jug overflows it is half full, and 7 hours before that it is one-quarter full, and 7 hours before that it is one-eighth full. Three times 7 is 21, so when we check the jug 24 hours before it overflows it is less than one-eighth full—mostly empty.

Now to make it vivid.

Suppose we start with 10 breeding pairs of bunnies living in a fenced meadow. There is no such thing as an infinite meadow: every meadow produces just so much food and water, and has just so much space. Suppose for the sake of the example that this is a large meadow that continuously produces enough food and water and contains enough space to support a thousand rabbits. Now the doubling time for populations of rabbits under ideal conditions is about 3 months, or 1 season, so they double their number 4 times per year. Thus after the first year our starting population of 20 rabbits has doubled 4 times, from 20 to 40, then to 80, then to 160, then to 320. So the second year starts with 320 rabbits. How many rabbits are there at the start of the third year?

The correct answer is 0. At the start of the third year there are no rabbits in the meadow at all. Not only that, the meadow is gone too. This is because the rabbits' population went into *overshoot*. In the first three months of the second year their numbers doubled from 320 to 640 and everything was going along fine. By midyear they had doubled again, to 1,280, and were eating up the available food faster than the meadow was regrowing it. Things were getting crowded too, but there was no panic; all the rabbits were still getting enough to eat, even though all the fresh, green shoots were gone and everybody had to eat the tough, older leaves and stems. But by the autumn the population had doubled again, to 2,560—far more than the meadow could support. Having eaten all the leaves, the rabbits ate the stems down to the ground. As they began to starve, in desperation they dug up the roots and ate those. In the end they ate each other. When the last rabbit died from starvation, it died in a desert.

This is a horrifying outcome, and fortunately nature has ways of preventing it. Coyotes, to begin with. Also, when food supplies become stressed the strongest and luckiest survive while others, weakened by hunger, succumb to predators and disease. In the real world populations of rabbits and of all animals fluctuate, sometimes wildly, from year to year, but over time tend to remain in rough balance.

Humans are an altogether different kind of animal. There is nothing to play the role of coyotes for us—we are the top of the food chain. We don't have to depend any longer on natural processes alone for our food, because with machinery and fertilizers and science we can extract from Mother Nature far more than she would give on her own. Disease too, while not conquered, is nothing like the scourge it once was. With the aid of technology we can fit vast numbers of us into comparatively small spaces. There are few natural forces left to constrain our numbers, and because of this our rate of population growth increased dramatically in the 20th century while our doubling time decreased from half a millennium to half a century.[144]

Humans are a different kind of animal, but not so different that the laws of mathematics don't apply to us. We live in a finite meadow, called the Earth. There is no other to which we might go. With all our knowledge and all our technology, there is still an absolute limit to how much this meadow can provide. We are not as prolific as rabbits, but our population is 7 billion and growing; our current doubling time is about 65 years.[145]

And we are in overshoot. It is not a question of *if* we will overshoot our environment, and it is not a question of *when*. We are in overshoot—right now. Sometime in the 1970s came the first year when the *ecological footprint* of humanity became so large that the impact on the planet was no longer sustainable.[146] Now, some 30 to 40 years later, we use up about 150% of the planet's yearly supply of resources every year.[147] In effect, if we apply the rabbits-in-the-meadow analogy, we are at the point of eating the stems.

There are several aspects that must be considered in measuring the degree and effects of human overshoot. They include the availability of food and water, disposal of waste, energy, biodiversity, and climate change. Each of these affects all the others.

Food

Predictions of mass starvation owing to overpopulation have been made for 200 years, but have not come to pass.[148] This is because our capacity to produce food has increased far beyond what was predicted. In the last 45 years in particular food production globally has more than doubled, keeping pace with the growth in population, even though the amount of land used for agriculture has scarcely increased at all.[149] This "green revolution," as it is called, is the result of four factors: Increased irrigation from underground aquifers, the increased use of manufactured fertilizers and pesticides, the use of machinery to more efficiently plant, harvest, process, and distribute food, and the development of higher-yielding, more disease- and insect-resistant crops.[150] [151] However, currently a billion people, 1 in 6, do not get sufficient nutrition, and an additional billion people are at risk.[152] Moreover, in order to keep pace with the population food production would have to double again in the next 35 years,[153] and this can't happen. Instead, food production is going to decline soon, and before long decline drastically.

One reason is that three of the four factors that made the green revolution possible cannot be sustained.

First, water. The United States' Great Plains, often called the breadbasket of the nation, produces enough grain for the country to be the world's biggest exporter of food.[154] However, this is possible in large part because of irrigation with water pumped from the Ogallala aquifer, an immense underground body of fresh water that stretches from South Dakota to Texas. Because of the geology and weather patterns of this region the aquifer is not replenished, and it is being used up so fast that in many areas water can no longer be pumped from it. It will be largely unusable for agriculture within 25 years.[155] This situation is mirrored across the globe, as aquifers that have driven increased food production in Europe, Asia, India, Africa, Australia, and the Middle East are drying up.[156] There is no replacement for water. As these aquifers run dry, food production will decline sharply.

Both the use of manufactured pesticides and fertilizers and the use of agricultural machinery depend on petroleum, which is a finite, non-renewable resource. Every calorie of food grown in the developed world requires many calories of fossil fuels to produce.[157] Global production of petroleum has either peaked or will peak within the decade. This does not mean that we will run out of oil; it means that every new barrel of oil will cost more to produce than the one before.[158] This is occurring at a time when the global demand for oil is increasing, so the average price of a barrel of oil is now more than four times what it was just 10 years ago, and continues to rise ever more steeply.[159] The result is that the cost of producing food is increasing, and will soon increase dramatically.[160] The increased price of oil was a principle factor in the 2007–2008 food price crisis that led to world-wide food riots and political instability,[161] a harbinger of events to come.

Fossil fuels are necessary not just for the increased food production of the last 45 years, but even to obtain previous levels of food production. This is because the fertility of the soils in the major food-producing regions has been depleted by industrial agriculture,[162] so the only way necessary nutrients can be supplied to growing crops is through the use of massive quantities of chemical fertilizers. For this reason, the role of fossil fuels in high-production agriculture cannot readily be filled by some other energy source. All the wind, solar, geothermal, and nuclear energy we could produce will not fertilize the soil.

Not only has the soil in which crops must be grown been depleted of its nutrients, the soil itself is disappearing. In the Great Plains about half of the original topsoil is gone, lost to erosion from industrial farming practices and poor soil management.[163] Current erosion of topsoil in the United States is occurring at a rate 10 times faster than nature can replace it, and this symptom of overshoot too is mirrored around the globe.[164] At the current rate of loss, *all* the Earth's topsoil will be gone in 70 years.[165]

A billion people rely on fish as their primary protein source, and fish accounts for about 20% of all protein in the human diet. However, the world's supply of fish has begun to collapse.[166] Three quarters of the world's fish stocks are in distress,[167] and populations of the largest food fish including tuna, swordfish, marlin, cod, halibut, and flounder have been decimated—literally, their numbers are a tenth of what they were in 1950.[168] The ocean ecosystem cannot recover unless there is a large *decrease* in human consumption of fish.

Meanwhile the production and consumption of meat is increasing worldwide—tripling in the last 40 years[169] [170]—and this is contributing to a net decline of food production in two ways. First, raising meat, either by grazing on land that could be producing food crops or in feedlots where the animals are fed grain and fodder, is a very inefficient way to produce food because the animals consume many times the value in food that they produce, and require many times the petroleum and water resources too.[171] Second, increased grazing in the 40% of global agricultural land that is arid has led to a process of desertification that is accelerating.

At least 10–20% of drylands have turned into deserts. The Sahara desert is expanding southward at a rate of nearly thirty miles per year.[172] In China, half a million square miles have turned to desert in the last 10 years.[173][174] This land will not recover within time-frames that are relevant to our civilization.[175]

Only 10% of the Earth's land can support agriculture.[176] The United Nations Food and Agriculture Organization reports that 25% of this land is highly degraded and that an additional 44% is slightly to moderately degraded.[177] There are no new frontiers, no fertile lands waiting to be put to use. Every part of the planet that can be exploited for human use is already being overexploited: humans are rapidly turning enormous regions that once supported agriculture into environments that cannot even support life. The meadow-to-desert conversion is well underway.

Water

Humans need fresh water. Without it, we die in a week. We need water that is uncontaminated by pollutants, disease organisms, and parasites. To sustain a civilized existence, we need extra water for sanitation, both for bodily cleanliness and to safely process human bodily wastes. At present about a billion people do not have adequate drinking water. They and an additional billion and a half people do not have adequate water for sanitation, a number that is increasing rapidly.[178] Half of the world's sick are sick because of inadequate water, and it is the leading cause of death for young children.[179] This is no longer just a third-world problem: 80% of the global population is "exposed to high levels of threat to water security."[180] That's 5.6 billion people.

Much of the current water crisis is owing to mismanagement, ignorance, and inadequate infrastructure in poorer parts of the world. However, human overshoot is becoming the dominating factor, with the needs of agriculture driving the shortages. About 70% of available fresh water goes to agriculture, and as noted above that resource is being depleted far faster than it can be renewed.[181] The depletion of aquifers results in reduced amounts of water flowing at the surface. Rivers are disappearing. The Yellow River in China, the Colorado River, and the Indus River in Pakistan no longer reach the ocean. This not only affects water availability for human consumption and use, but has grave implications for the ecosystems and biodiversity that depend on these waters.[182]

Waste

Each of 315 million Americans generates, on average, nearly 4 1/2 pounds of waste every day. Together we produce about 250 million tons every year. This is three times the amount we produced 50 years ago.[183] Although Americans produce more waste per person than in any other country, the rest of the world is catching up. Precise estimates are difficult, but total solid waste production world-wide is in the billions of tons. The World Bank recently warned that this portends an economic and environmental burden as catastrophic as climate change.[184]

This waste is mostly just dumped, although some is incinerated or buried. It is a primary contributor to environmental degradation including loss of arable land, air and water pollution (including poisoning of groundwater from leaching), disruption of local ecosystems, and global warming.[185] Millions of tons are dumped into the world's oceans each year, destroying marine habitats such as coral reefs. Dozens of large pieces and many thousands of tiny pieces of plastic litter are floating on every square mile of ocean.[186] This plastic absorbs non-water-soluble poisons such as DDT, so when it is ingested by fish these poisons enter the food chain.[187] Recently vast islands of floating trash have been discovered around the globe, some larger than the state of Texas.[188]

Even greater damage to fresh and ocean-water systems is caused by agricultural pollution, especially excess nitrogen. Areas like the 8,000 square mile dead-zone in the Gulf of Mexico at the mouth of the Mississippi River, caused by fertilizer runoff from as far away as Minnesota, are becoming commonplace.[189]

The Mississippi River itself, one of the great rivers of the world, has been destroyed as a functioning ecosystem[190]—it is now just the biggest of several national sewer pipes emptying into the sea. It is difficult to find any stream or other body of water in the world that is unaffected by waste, a fact closely related to the threat to water security for the majority of the world's population.

Energy
There are just a few sources of energy on Earth: nuclear, geothermal, tidal, and everything else—and the everything else is solar. Wind power is really solar energy, as is hydroelectric. Most importantly, all fossil fuels are solar energy, banked by the planet over vast geological time frames.

Between 100 and 135 billion metric tons of petroleum have been extracted and used since 1850.[191] About 190 billion tons remains, which at current rates of extraction is about 60 years' worth. However, only 30% of the remaining oil is conventional light crude. The remainder consists of much-harder-to-extract-and-process heavy crude and tar sands.[192] Although there are many ways to replace both the energy and materials that crude oil provides, there is no way to replace petroleum that will allow us to consume resources at the rate we now do. This is because petroleum is a uniquely *concentrated* form of chemical energy with many important properties:

- It is lightweight,
- It is easy to store and transport,
- It is comparatively safe to handle,
- It releases its energy as slowly or as quickly as almost any application requires, and
- It costs (while the light oil lasts) little to bring it to market.

One gallon of gasoline will do about the work of 13 kilowatt hours of electricity, taking into account typical efficiencies.[193]

However, the gallon of gas weighs 7 pounds and can be held in a tank costing a few bucks, and the bank of batteries to hold 13 kilowatt hours ready for immediate use weighs 435 pounds and costs $8,000.[194][195] Also, those batteries require several hours to charge fully. If you wanted to create those 13 kilowatt hours yourself using a typical household solar installation rated at 5 kilowatts, it would take your system several hours on a sunny day—or several cloudy days—to do so, longer if you live in a northern state.[196]

Even on a very large scale electricity is two to three times more expensive to produce with renewable sources than with fossil fuels.[197] In theory, nuclear fission can be used to produce electricity as cheaply as fossil fuels can, and without the greenhouse gas emissions. In practice however, avoiding the risk of catastrophic accidents such as happened at Chernobyl and Fukushima makes the costs of constructing, maintaining, and eventually decommissioning nuclear energy plants prohibitive[198][199][200]—even leaving aside the horrific long-term risk to people and the environment they represent—which is why countries around the world are abandoning their nuclear energy plans.

But even supposing the cost of generating electricity could be held low, perhaps by some yet undiscovered or unproven technology like nuclear fusion, we still face an unavoidable crisis. Using electricity to create the kinds of fuels and materials necessary to sustain intensive agriculture would still require far greater time, effort, and money than simply pumping oil out of the ground and refining it. Moreover, such fuels and materials themselves can only be created—absent fossil fuels—from agricultural products. Replacing even a small fraction of our current fuel and fertilizer requirements with renewable sources diverts a significant percentage of agricultural output away from food production; diverting 25% of the United States' corn crop in 2007 to ethanol production resulted in 6 billion gallons of ethanol, an amount equal to less than 5% of all the gasoline we used that year.[201] Worse, when the petroleum products used to grow the corn to make the ethanol are figured in, the net gain was at best 2 billion gallons of ethanol, and some analyses suggest there was no net gain at all, but a net loss.[202] It isn't possible to grow enough to create enough fuel and fertilizer to allow us to grow enough.

A century or so ago humanity stumbled upon a great prize: the accumulated store of eons-worth of solar energy in the form of petroleum and other fossil fuels. This discovery is the primary reason for the sudden and rapid rise in our numbers. But we didn't understand soon enough that it was not just a prize but a trap; that once the store was spent there could be no replacement. There is now no escape. Within the lifetimes of those now living humanity will revert to a level of consumption that has not been seen in the developed world for 100 years.

Biodiversity
Comparatively few of the millions of species of plants and animals are, by themselves, of obvious importance to humans and their survival. However, every species of plant or animal is part of a complex web of relationships that sustains a stable ecosystem. Changing those relationships by reducing or removing any one or more species can have far-reaching consequences, and it is impossible to predict at what point such interference will cause the ecosystem to break down.[203] The destruction of any ecosystem is a direct threat to humans because we depend on healthy ecosystems for processes that are essential to our survival. Some of the most important roles that ecosystems play are:[204]

- To replenish and fertilize the soil,
- To filter and purify water and recharge aquifers,
- To absorb carbon and regulate the climate,
- To pollinate food crops,
- To sustain fisheries, and
- To absorb and recycle waste.

From 2001 to 2005 the United Nations sponsored the Millennium Ecosystem Assessment, a wide-ranging study involving more than a thousand scientists. The assessment concluded that 60% of ecosystems are degraded or unsustainably managed.[205] As a result, the current rate of species extinction is 1,000 times higher than normal.[206] This rate is consistent with those of the five previous "Great Extinctions" in the fossil record, brief periods when diversity was reduced by more than 75%, the most recent of which 60 million years ago wiped out the dinosaurs. Absent a dramatic turnaround in the impact of humanity on the planet, we are witnessing the sixth Great Extinction.[207] The unavoidable result is the collapse of the ecosystems on which human civilization depends.

Climate Change

The Earth is not a stable environment but a profoundly complex system undergoing continual change. The present temperate climate in particular is neither permanent nor even typical; even the recent geological past has seen periods of both warmer and much colder weather. The constant changes in climate are owing to many factors, from the behavior of the sun to the influence of physical and biological processes on Earth.

Presently the Earth is getting warmer. What is different this time is that it is getting warmer much faster than can be explained by any known natural process. Each of the last 11 years has been one of the warmest 12 on record, and 2012 has thus far (this was written in August) been the hottest year ever recorded. This can only be explained by the influence of humanity[208 209] and is therefore also a feature of overshoot.

Since the start of the 21st century temperatures on land each year have been between 1 1/4 and 1 3/4 degrees fahrenheit above the average for the 20th century. The same period has seen a marked increase in destructive weather events such as floods, droughts, and storms, and these are now confirmed to be a result of the higher temperatures.[210 211] Additional visible consequences are record melts of polar ice, the vanishing of glaciers, shifting habitats and behaviors of many animal species, changes in seasonal vegetation growth and habitat, and rising sea levels.[212]

Every climate model predicts that the temperature will continue to increase rapidly at least in the medium term, and there is no indication that any effective program to prevent or even mitigate continued forcing of the climate by human activity is politically possible.[213] The probable consequences for those now living include:[214][215]

- Greater extremes of both hot and cold weather, as seasonal oscillations increase in amplitude.
- More severe flooding, more severe droughts, and larger and more intense forest fires.
- More intense storms, in particular more intense tropical cyclones, including Atlantic hurricanes.
- Reduced water resources in semi-arid areas such as the western United States.
- Shifting wildlife habitats resulting in accelerated extinctions.
- Movement of tropical diseases such as malaria into temperate regions.
- Frequent and widespread crop loss.
- A rise in average sea levels of at least several inches, up to over a foot.
- Mass displacements and migrations of human populations.

These effects are all, for practical purposes, permanent and irreversible. Other more abrupt and catastrophic effects such as are known to have happened in the past are also possible. Although no single one appears probable, they all are consistent with the expected shift in climate.[216]

- Runaway climate change, in which higher temperatures cause a sudden release of large amounts of greenhouse gases which cause yet higher temperatures, leading to a large amplification of all of the above effects.

- A large-scale shift in ocean currents, completely and permanently disrupting all established weather patterns and leading to climatic and ecological chaos.

- Runaway forest fires in the tropical zones, resulting in a severe loss of carbon-sequestering, oxygen-releasing plant-life and dramatically increasing the greenhouse effect.

The one certain consequence of climate change is increased stress to already overburdened natural and agricultural systems. The very recent past provides a number of examples, such as the severe world-wide droughts in most of the last 10 years (causing major food shortages) and an unrelenting series of severe floods, storms, and forest fires in the United States and elsewhere around the world during the same period. In 2012 we saw record-setting droughts, with serious implications for the global food supply.[217] Global warming is an overshoot accelerant: it magnifies, exacerbates, and hastens all the other effects of human overpopulation.

* * * * *

It is hard to summarize the consequences of human overshoot, and even harder to draw specific conclusions about its final outcome. As the physicist Niels Bohr remarked, prediction is difficult, especially of the future. However, if you see someone stacking blocks one atop another into a high tower, and if that tower gets many times higher than the base that supports it, you can say with certainty that if blocks keep being added it will topple over. You can't say exactly *when* it will topple. You can't say in what direction. You can't say whether the collapse will begin at the bottom or somewhere in the middle. But—you can still know with a certainty that it must fall, and fall soon.

It is also true that the sheer number of people on Earth is not by itself what determines the severity of our overshoot; it is the average rate of consumption multiplied by the population. In this respect Americans have much to answer for, because our ecological footprint is *several times larger* than most of the rest of humanity's.[218] If everyone on Earth consumed as much as the average American, all would have perished long before now.

So there are two things we can say with certainty. First, the size of the human population will drop very substantially. Estimates of the carrying capacity of the planet vary widely, but those estimates that take account of the facts presented here are much lower than the current population.[219] When we also take into account the severe degradation of the planet's ecosystems that is likely yet to occur, we must be even more pessimistic.[220] How the drop in population will occur, when it will begin to occur, how long it will last, and what the population will be afterward is impossible to know. It may be disease, or war, or (the default) famine. It is likely to be a combination of things. But it cannot be avoided.

The second thing we can say with certainty is that the rate of human consumption must decrease to a small fraction of the current average in the developed world. In particular, anything like the current consumer culture will be quite impossible.

Human ecological overshoot is the defining fact of life on Earth for the foreseeable future. This issue doesn't just dwarf other issues; it absorbs every issue—political, cultural, economic, and environmental—into itself. Far too many people are still asking how we can avoid the consequences of overshoot. This is like someone who is already falling asking how to avoid hitting the ground. The right question is, how can we best cope with and mitigate the consequences? How do we shape our lives to fit the future we have made for ourselves? Or rather, not our lives, for that die is cast. What can we do now so that our children's children's children may *have* a world to live in, in freedom, dignity, and peace?

5 Voting For, Voting Against

The United States is a republic, so in principle it is the people who are in charge. In practice, as shown in Chapter 3, it has not worked out that way. Nonetheless, because we remain a formal democracy there remains a possibility—a potential—that is as tantalizing as it is breathtaking: the people *could* reclaim their government.

There are effective barriers in place to prevent this:

- Voting is deliberately made difficult.
- Voters are heavily propagandized.
- Voters' choices are limited.

Because of these barriers only slightly more than half of Americans who could vote actually do so in presidential election years, fewer than half in other national elections, and far fewer in local or state-level elections that are held apart from national elections. Voter participation has steadily declined since 1960. Those who fail to vote, when polled, cite the difficulty of voting as the primary cause.[221]

Erecting hurdles on the way to the voting booth is an American tradition, from the poll taxes, literacy tests, and good-character tests of the Jim Crow era to today's voter id laws and proof-of-residency requirements. Polling places are often put in locations that disadvantage voters who don't have a car. Voting is held on a workday, forcing voters to miss work or try to fit voting in before or after work, a time when the polling places are busiest and the lines to vote in crowded urban districts can be hours long.[222]

37

Voter suppression begins well before polling day, however: the fact that Americans must *register* to vote enables a number of mechanisms to block them. Registration requirements and restrictions vary significantly from state to state, and change frequently, so voters tend to be poorly informed about their eligibility to register as well as what process to follow. Also, deadlines to register come a month before election day and vary from state to state, so many miss their chance to register without knowing it, especially young and first-time voters. States are not required to notify voters of their registration status, so voters are unsure of whether they may vote come election day, or what will happen if they try to vote when they aren't pre-qualified.[223]

The 2012 election was especially remarkable for the boldness of the attack on voting, an attack coordinated at the national level but aimed at individual state laws.[224][225] In 2011 alone 14 state legislatures enacted a total of 25 laws to restrict voter registration, increase documentation and residency requirements for registration, enhance disenfranchisement of former convicts, restrict early or absentee voting, and require government-issued photo ID at the polling place.[226][227] Some states purged their voter rolls on spurious grounds, disenfranchising many voters without their knowledge and forcing them to meet new, onerous registration requirements.[228][229][230] The "voting fraud" problem that serves as the public rationale for erecting these barriers to democracy does not exist.[231] Rather it is clear that these measures are meant to deflect the threat to elite interests that broad participation at the polls might represent.[232][233]

Supposing you run the gauntlet and cast your vote, there is a good chance you are deceived about what you are voting for. In the 2010 national elections the majority of conservative voters believed that healthcare reform will increase the deficit, that the economy was shrinking rather than growing, that the stimulus included no tax cuts, and that scientists do not largely agree about the existence of climate change. In the same election, most liberal voters believed that the Chamber of Commerce was spending foreign money to support Republican candidates, that troop levels in Afghanistan were not increased during the Obama administration, and that Democratic legislators did not support the TARP bank bailout. All of these beliefs are contrary to the facts.[234] Similar findings have been reported in the past. In the presidential election in 2000 significant numbers of voters were confused about such basic matters as which candidate was more conservative and which party controlled the legislature.[235] [236]

If enough voters are confused about the candidates and policies they are voting for then the entire electorate is disenfranchised. But voter confusion is not accidental, and it is not owing to lack of interest or to intellectual incapacity. It is deliberately imposed. Like all other advertising, the information that voters are exposed to is meant to hinder their critical faculties, place a distorted frame on their perceptions, and appeal to their prejudices. The U.S. presidential campaigns alone were predicted to spend $3 billion dollars on political ads in the 2012 cycle,[237] while political action committees and other partisan organizations spent far more. This money is spent not to inform but to persuade, and it is being spent on the most effective public relations that money can buy. *Obama for America,* the president's 2008 campaign, won top national and international prizes from advertising industry organizations for its effectiveness.[238] [239]

Behind and superior to the major party campaigns is big media's role in setting the agenda:[240] [241] [242] the issues to be fought over and—critically—the issues to be left undiscussed. So in the latest election cycle voters were trained to treat the deficit as the paramount economic concern, the "threats" from Iran and China as the top international issue, and women's reproductive health choices as the top social issue.[243] Of these, only the third has any connection with voters' interests, as opposed to elite interests. Off the menu: the military-security establishment that absorbs over half of income tax revenues, the capture and rape of the economy by an international financial elite, the sacrifice of individual privacy and civil liberties on the altar of the War on Terror, the collapse of our civic commons[244][245][246] and disintegration of the physical infrastructures[247] on which any long-term economic recovery depends, and the poverty and poor prospects that define the lives of a majority of Americans. As Jim Naureckas once put it, writing in FAIR:

> When you're exposed to network TV news, it's always good to bear in mind that you're watching millionaires working for billionaires, telling stories whose main purpose (from an economic perspective) is to get you to hold still long enough for corporate advertisements to rearrange your value system.[248]

The first tool of propaganda is partisanship, and it is unsurprising that the top social issue on the agenda—abortion—is one of the most polarized issues among voters. Partisanship is the mechanism by which voters are most often deceived, because their understanding of the facts is easily distorted when such distortions fit the biases and narratives they have already adopted.[249][250][251] In addition, partisanship makes voters less likely to pay attention to or be influenced by new information.[252] A highly polarized and partisan electorate is a neutralized electorate, provided approximate numerical balance between the parties is maintained—a dynamic ensured by a two-party system in which capture of the political center ("center" as defined by the agenda-setters) is key to success.[253]

The partisan duopoly exploits popular political impulses in ways that ensure those impulses don't threaten the system. Corporate-media news sources are careful to maintain an artificial standard of "balance" in any story focused on political issues, even when it requires treating isolated, unsupported opinions on an equal footing with readily verified facts.[254][255][256] False balance doesn't just avoid undermining partisan narratives, it places a partisan frame on issues that then limits what can be considered legitimate points of view. Any view not within the defined spectrum is automatically "extreme" and "unserious," and hence unworthy of public attention. In this way the "center" of political opinion, the views that count as moderate, can be adjusted over time to suit elite interests.[257]

Elections are presented as a competition between opposing teams, like a national sporting event not much different than the Super Bowl or the World Series, and voters are kept focused on how their team is doing and the latest indicators of partisan advantage. Local and state-level races become the focus of national media only insofar as they are relevant to the national outcome, offer scandal, or become the focus of fierce partisan competition; local media ("local" in the sense of coverage, not ownership) largely ignore them too.[258] News coverage of any issue that is relevant to voters' choices in the election—already limited by the boundaries of the set agenda—becomes further limited by the need to emphasize the role of the issue in determining the outcome of the competition, emphasis that often comes with a large dose of false balance.

Candidates and policy proposals that don't conform to the partisan narratives are considered fringe, and denied news coverage or a podium in the debates. Third parties such as the Greens, the Libertarians, or the Socialists are actually called "spoilers"[259]— literally people who ruin the game for everybody else. Any votes they get are said to have been "stolen" from the major party candidates, and the votes themselves are said to be "wasted." The harsh language used to describe any deviation from the partisan dynamic indicates how firmly established that dynamic is; most voters have completely internalized it, and are unaware that other ways of approaching the conduct of American politics might be rational, or even possible.

Partisanship inexorably increases.[260] Those who vote don't

vote for things. A partisan vote is fundamentally a *vote against* because a partisan vote is about winning, and you can't win if your
opponent does. Political discourse in the United States is therefore dominated by the superficial, the personal, and the polarizing.
Above all it is increasingly negative.[261] [262] It has to be, because
that is how you motivate people to v*ote against.* The resulting
political environment is hostile to constructive debate of the kind
that forges consensus and fosters leadership. We are left with an
electorate whose representatives are unable clearly to articulate the
nation's problems, much less imagine their solutions.

Taken together, the obstacles to voting that reduce turnout, the
propaganda that keeps likely voters misinformed about and distracted from the issues that affect their lives, and the constraints
on discourse and political action enforced by a duopoly of parties
that are distinct in far fewer respects than they are identical (and
in nothing more so than the interests they serve)—these defects in
American democracy neutralize the ballot box as a tool for self-
government. There is no other tool for self-government. Without
it the notion that our government is "of and by the people" is a
fiction, convenient to no one but those whose hands are on the real
levers of power.

6 The Good American

When I was quite young it was common for people to indulge in sanctimonious talk about the "good German" in World War II. Such conversations took as given that the Third Reich was evil and that the good German faced a paradox of loyalties, having to choose between the sin of participating in the evil or the sin of betraying his people. I have been alarmed to hear echoes of that facile discussion in my fellow Americans' debates about our own country. One hears these echoes from those who defend our endless wars, boundless consumption, and childish outlook as well as from those who condemn them.

The defenders make a fetish of chauvinistic patriotism, treating principled opposition as betrayal. But many critics, some of whom I admire, are also simplistic, equating patriotism itself with betrayal—that is, with betrayal of those universal values that are outraged by the country's behavior.[263] [264]

My own experience has the virtue of being both familiar to me and instructive: I did not find out that I was an American until I went abroad. Before then and throughout my youth, tutored as I was by internationalist relatives and schooled in universal values, I imagined that I was broader than my mere country of origin and that my cultural identity was mine to create. My thinking was that I would be sort of British in my sensibilities but retain the rugged individualism associated with the American west—and be tempered by "eastern wisdom." I would like to think these youthful conceits would be behind me now anyway, if not because they were conceits then at least because they were youthful, even if I had never left Colorado. But they withered swiftly when I was immersed in cultures that hadn't made me. I found out I was an American for good or ill—for good and ill—not at home but in a German church, an English pub, and the streets of Rome.

I don't mean to say that I stopped being an internationalist or stopped professing universal values. Quite the opposite. But I ceased to suppose that my identity was something I could simply conjure up. I learned that as a human being I am the product of a particular country and a particular culture; I can no more walk away from it than I can walk away from my skin.

So ordinary patriotism is not jingoism, it is not totemism or rooting for the home team or any such superficial or bigoted loyalty. It is an acknowledgement that we only exist in virtue of our being bred and sustained by something much larger than ourselves, but particular and consisting of many selves past and present, that forms the linguistic, political, social, and cultural matrix of our lives. It is the love of home *because* it is home—because it is who we are. It is not one loyalty among others, but the very framework that makes loyalties possible.

So in considering our situation as Americans and thinking over our obligations and future courses of action, the first thing we cannot propose is, "stop being an American." Anyone, including an American, can and should be much, much more than an American, but there are 315 million of us who won't be less. I am also not going to try to enumerate the ethical obligations that are common to all human beings. The universal values and their commitments that are acknowledged by educated and emancipated people of all cultures I naturally take to be binding upon my own people. *Homo sum,* as Terence wrote; I am a man, I deem nothing common to humankind foreign to me.[265]

I am concerned here rather to identify those obligations specific to American citizens at this time. I have set forth our most serious challenges. The situation is grave, the eyes of the world turn upon us in doubt and fear, and the future hangs in the balance—in many ways not so much *what* the future will be, but *whether*.

We cannot even begin until we have put away our pride. Americans imbibe American exceptionalism from birth; it sustains all our national myths. *We* are the oldest democracy.[266] *We* are the defenders of freedom.[267] *We* are the beacon of hope for the world.[268] In the words of a recent president, we are the world's only "indispensable nation."[269]

The belief that oneself is exceptional is the deadbolt on the prison of hypocrisy. Americans must reexamine themselves as a people, read their history and the canon of their deeds with a clear eye, and confess:

- That we have been enemies of freedom and extinguishers of hope in dark episodes too numerous for pride to bear.
- That our appetite for lands, resources, wealth, and power is and always has been rapacious.
- That our economy and our culture are not free, but are alike captives of a corrupt system of state capitalism not legitimated by the principles upon which our nation was founded.

Above all, Americans must confront the ultra-violence that has colored their nation's every historic moment, from the campaigns of extermination and the blood-soaked fields of the warring states to the irradiated hellscapes of Hiroshima and Nagasaki, the rape and devastation of Iraq. We have flooded the world with weapons of every obscene kind and slain whom it suits us indifferently, until the very stink of death is branded "Made in America."

If we cannot acknowledge our failings, if we cannot find the national humility necessary to admission and contrition, then we surely lack the strength for what must come after. Only when we shed the golem-costume of imagined greatness and return to the sinews of our own body can the real heavy-lifting begin.

That heavy-lifting begins with revision. We must revisit the principles and purposes of government enunciated in our founding documents, and identify the ways in which they are not fulfilled by our present political, social, and economic institutions. As often before in our history, we must confront the reality that our democracy remains uncompleted. The founders gave us much, but left much for us to do.

In the past and within the framework of our constitutional system we righted many institutional wrongs. We abolished slavery, scrubbed our laws free of the stain of racism, extended the vote—once restricted to white men of property—to every citizen, and rescued the aged and the infirm from the tragedy of destitution and the young from the prisons of ignorance and exploitation. These pillars of a just society were in every instance built in the face of determined opposition from its most privileged members.

The challenges we now confront—the steep decline in our civic culture and commons, the collapse of our ecosystem, the financial ruin of working Americans, and the frustration of democratic self-government—all are symptoms of an institutional failing that has long been recognized: political democracy cannot survive without economic democracy. This fact was already brought into sharp focus by the economic storm that devastated America 70 years ago, after which there were many efforts to extend the democratic ideal to the realm of economics. Proposals like the 40-hour workweek, the minimum wage, mandatory overtime,[270] and a progressive tax code[271] were successful. Others, such as Franklin Delano Roosevelt's Economic Bill of Rights,[272] were not.

As shown in Chapter 3, after a period in the 1950's and 60's of comparative economic equality (and concomitant stability) the country got suckered all over again. We are hammered now by the same old truth: our government cannot remain accountable to the people when an unaccountable financial elite controls the economy. Oligarchy and democracy will have no accord; inevitably, one must go.

As my mathematician friends like to say, a solution exists. It is difficult to see because we have been trained to not see it, constrained in our thinking by a false dichotomy between two discreditable theories of freedom.

The first theory holds that when the individual is completely unfettered in the quest for personal wealth, everybody prospers. The second theory holds that unless economic activity is tightly controlled, the majority can never be free from exploitation. The first theory, *laissez-faire* capitalism, embodies a quasi-religious faith that greed is a virtue and that a benevolent "invisible hand" will shield humanity from any economic catastrophe. The second theory, state socialism, is the rationalist fallacy that civilization can prosper within the enforced limits of a stick-figure model of human affairs. Neither theory accords with known facts. Greed is not a virtue, but a sin. It is neither accumulation nor influence that fulfill a human life, but service and community—truths affirmed by every major religion and every respectable philosophy. At the same time, human prosperity cannot be designed, legislated, or imposed. The economy of human existence is irreducibly complex, so that any system that seeks centrally to direct it inevitably breaks it, causing greater want and certain strife—truths affirmed by history.

Economic democracy is the synthesis that bridges the gap between unrepentant capitalism and unenlightened socialism. We do not want a chaotic jungle of warring weeds, nor do we want regimented rows of the same drear seedlings, but a richly planted garden alive with variety and interest and room for good things to prosper. This outcome is never final, but an eternal dance to balance a kaleidoscope of evolving interests. Only a living government continually deriving its powers from the people it governs can succeed.

I am not qualified, nor is it my purpose here, to propose specific policies, but the outlines of necessary change are apparent from our situation. We are in an emergency. Obscene economic inequality and exploitation, rampant consumption, and pervasive, institutionalized corruption must be abruptly corrected. The rule of law must be restored. The military industrial complex must be dismantled. Democratic participation must be facilitated, not obstructed. Enormous positive change can be achieved with a few simple steps, such as publicly funding elections and making election day a holiday. Other necessary steps, such as taking monetary policy out of the hands of private banking moguls, will need sage counsel to do correctly.

What is above all clear is that until the power that government derives from its people includes control of our economic institutions there can be no economic democracy, and therefore, before long, no democracy at all. This is a challenge made greater by the fact that the most powerful economic interests dominate our government while operating to a large extent unconstrained by our nation's borders or our people's sovereignty.

It is for this reason that revision is an empty exercise without the will for revolution. I do not shy from the word: revolution was identified by the founders as a continuing obligation of American patriotism. The Virginian Thomas Jefferson wrote, "Experience has shown that even under the best forms of government those entrusted with power have, in time, and by slow operations, perverted it into tyranny,"[273] and he is widely believed to have said that "every generation needs a new revolution." But I also do not propose revolution cavalierly. I would almost rather say "restoration" than "revolution," because it is a rare revolution that supplants a power system with one more just, particularly if there is deliberate violence. But it is clear that we are past being able merely to correct the course of many of our present institutions. The restoration of the democratic principles of government that are our rightful inheritance demands radical structural change in the economic order. Those who hold the levers of power will not surrender their advantage, however unjust that advantage, without struggle.

I am not calling for overthrow of the government—in the United States the people *are* the government. I'm calling for us to start acting like it. We must reach out and claim what is ours. The Constitution, whatever its flaws, has proven a sound instrument in the past for achieving revolutionary change, and it can do so again. There is nothing in it that establishes the Republican and Democratic parties, or billionaire political donors, or banks too big to fail as necessary components of our democracy. There is nothing in it to prevent the people making whatever changes under its authority are needed to meet the current crisis, however revolutionary those changes might be, however much they discomfit the comfortable.

Nothing finally to prevent the people—except the people. We can only succeed by internalizing some difficult truths and making some unexpected sacrifices. Some of us need to renounce our greed and join the human race—or be dealt with. Many of us need to put away our childish things, our tweets and our teams and our shopping, wake up, and smell the world burning. Most of us need to wean ourselves from the flashy screen that sells our eyeballs as a commodity to the propagandists, and recover our native capacity for thought. All of us need to recognize that without our immediate and focused engagement we stand to lose everything, for we and our children could well be the last bunnies in the meadow.

Above all, each American must accept the burden of citizenship. Our patriotic obligation is not to grab a gun and shoot the enemy, but to grasp the hand of our neighbor, acknowledge our differences without ill will, and search together for the common ground on which our shared future will stand. As voters it means not being schooled in the faults of the opposition but in the issues that face us and the policies we support to address them. Americans must *exercise* their citizenship; it is not a passive role, but a very active one. To be called an *activist* should be an acclamation of civic honor.

And when election day comes it means *voting for*, not against. This will be hardest of all for some; it means accepting that the other side might win because one's own side was divided. But it is time to give up sides. Voting against is a devil's bargain, and a lazy one. It is the very mechanism by which the American electorate is today disenfranchised. Loyalty is a virtue, but not brand loyalty, and especially not in politics. Politicians are practical people—they need you to vote for them. Only when Americans are able to discern the interests a candidate really represents can they know what they are voting for. And only when Americans are informed and vote the issues can they hold elected leaders to account for what they do.

With the revolution must come a re-engagement with the world. Properly managed we will remain a wealthy country, and with the revolution we will have again the influence of democratic example. But we must be mindful of our sins and willing to earn the trust and friendship of others, not least by showing, in Jefferson's words, a "decent respect for the opinions of mankind."

Re-engagement is critical not just for the rehabilitation of our world citizenship. Humanity faces a crisis of inexpressible severity, one that will spawn a thousand offspring in wars, famines, migrations, and civil strife. Without global cooperation and leadership there is little hope that our world will even be recognizable in another generation.

There remains only one way Americans can provide leadership: we must demonstrate to the world that democracy can turn a future filled with want into a future of dignity and promise. We must redesign prosperity into a feature of stewardship rather than of exploitation, taking only what we restore. After all, the world can (and will) get on just fine when humanity is gone—but we cannot get on without the world.

Now, let us take up our burden together.

Notes

[1]Declaration of Independence of the United States. Thomas Jefferson, 1776. "Governments [derive] their just powers from the consent of the governed."

[2]US Government census data.

[3]*World Population Policies 2005*, United Nations Department of Economic and Social Affairs, Population Division.

[4]*US Military and Clandestine Operations in Foreign Countries—1798–Present.* Global Policy Forum. Dec. 2005 (www.globalpolicy.org /empire/history/interventions.htm).

[5]*Timeline of US Military Actions and War, 1775-Present.* American Experience. Public Broadcasting System. (www.pbs.org /wgbh/amex/warletters/timeline/index.html)

[6]*Indian Wars.* Wikipedia. (en.wikipedia.org /wiki/Indian_Wars)

[7]*Convention on the Prevention and Punishment of the Crime of Genocide.* Wikipedia. (en.wikipedia.org /wiki/Genocide_Convention)

[8]*International Criminal Court.* Wikipedia. (en.wikipedia.org /wiki/International_criminal_court)

[9]Judgment of the ICJ in Nicaragua v. United States of America, 27 June 1986. (www.icj-cij.org /docket/index.php?sum=367&code=nus&p1=3&p2=3&case=70&k=66&p3=5)

[10]United Nations. Repertory of Practice of United Nations Organs, Supplement 7, Volume VI, Article 94. http://untreaty.un.org /cod/repertory/art94/english/rep_supp7_vol6-art94_e._advance.pdf.

[11]*Ottowa Treaty.* Wikipedia. (en.wikipedia.org /wiki/Ottawa_Treaty)

[12]*Cluster Munitions: Key Facts.* Cluster Munition Coalition. (www.stopclustermunitions.org /dokumenti/dokument.asp?id=108)

[13]*Circle of Impact: The Fatal Footprint of Cluster Munitions on People and Communities.* Handicap International. (en.handicapinternational.be /download/Circle_of_impact_EXECUTIVE_SUMMARY.pdf)

[14]*Census Counts 100,000 Contractors in Iraq.* The Washington Post. (www.washingtonpost.com /wp-dyn/content/article/2006/12/04/AR2006120401311.html.)

[15]*Risks of Afghan War Shift From Soldiers To Contractors.* The New York Times. (www.nytimes.com /2012/02/12/world/asia/afghan-war-risks-are-

shifting-to-contractors.html?_r=1&ref=privatemilitarycompanies)

[16]*Private Military Contractors and the Law. Human Rights Watch.* (hrw.org /english/docs/2004/05/05/iraq8547_txt.htm)

[17]Davidson, Osha Gray. *Contract to Torture.* Salon.com. 9 Aug 2004 (dir.salon.com /story/news/feature/2004/08/09/abu_ghraib/index.html)

[18]The most famous American-sponsored terrorist at present is Luis Posada Carriles, a Cuban exile known to have masterminded the bombing of Cubana flight 455 in 1976, killing all 73 people aboard. He is also responsible for additional bombings, assassination plots, and other crimes. He was trained by the CIA at the School of the Americas in 1961, and remained on the payroll of that agency intermittently from the early 1960's well into the 1990's. In 2005 he was arrested for entering the United States illegally. However, the U.S. refused an extradition request by Venezuela, the immigration charges were dismissed, and as of this writing Carriles is free and living in Miami. His case can be reviewed on the National Security Archives website maintained at George Washington University: http://www.gwu.edu /ñsarchiv/NSAEBB/NSAEBB153/index.htm.

[19]The United States was the first to design, build, and use nuclear weapons, and has always been first with new technologies. There are at least a dozen sites in the United States still actively engaged in the research or production of nuclear weapons, most notably at the Los Alamos, Sandia, Livermore, and Oak Ridge national laboratories. The United States cancelled its biological weapons program in 1969 and ratified the international Biological Weapons Convention in 1975, but it continues "defensive" research—greatly expanded since 2001—into biological agents at Fort Detrick, Maryland and at many government-sponsored labs around the country, and it has distributed "samples" of biological agents to allies around the world, including to Saddam Hussein during the Reagan and first Bush administrations. The United States renounced the use of chemical weapons in 1969, and as of this writing has nearly 90% of its original stockpile, but it has failed to meet the deadlines specified in the treaty for completing their destruction (en.wikipedia.org /wiki/United_States_and_weapons_of_mass_destruction). In addition, it has continued to use white phosphorous—commonly considered a chemical weapon—as an anti-personnel weapon in violation of Protocol III of the Geneva Conventions (which it refuses to sign) (en.wikipedia.org /wiki/White_phosphorus_use_in_Iraq).

[20]Examples when commanders may request presidential approval for use of theater nuclear weapons include "to counter potentially overwhelming adversary conventional forces," to obtain "rapid and favorable war termination

on US terms," and "to ensure success of US and multinational operations." Joint Publication 3-12, Doctrine for Joint Nuclear Operations, Joint Chiefs of Staff of the United States, 15 March 2005.

[21]Hiroshima and Nagasaki, Japan, on August 6th and 9th respectively, 1945, resulting in the deaths of nearly a quarter of a million civilian inhabitants of those cities (en.wikipedia.org /wiki/Hiroshima_and_Nagasaki).

[22]*Obama Order Sped Up Wave of Cyberattacks Against Iran.* New York Times. 1 June 2012. (www.nytimes.com /2012/06/01/world/middleeast/obama-ordered-wave-of-cyberattacks-against-iran.html?pagewanted=all)

[23]"Our forces will be strong enough to dissuade potential adversaries from pursuing a military build-up in hopes of surpassing, or equaling, the power of the United States." National Security Strategy of the United States, Sept. 2002 (nssarchive.us/?page_id=32). This document also explicitly reserves to the president the right to conduct "preemptive" military operations anywhere in the world at his sole discretion. In concert with the Department of Defense's governing military doctrine (since 1996) of Rapid Dominance, better known as "shock and awe," which calls for the physical obliteration of any opponent's "means of communication, transportation, food production, water supply, and other aspects of infrastructure," this statement put the nations of the world on notice that the U.S. shall not be challenged, on penalty of utter destruction (viz. Iraq). In 2010 the Obama administration replaced this detailed but controversial document with a new "National Security Strategy" declaration consisting largely of vague platitudes, clearly meant for public consumption, but which also emphasizes the United States continuing commitment to maintain military "superiority." (www.whitehouse.gov /sites/default/files/rss_viewer/national_security_strategy.pdf, page 14)

[24]According to figures released in 1995 by Vietnam's Ministry of Labor, War Invalids and Social Affairs, two million North Vietnamese civilians died in their war with the United States, and two million additionally perished in South Vietnam. Most of these four million may reasonably be assumed to have perished from direct U.S. military action, most from deliberate massive bombing of civilian populations. These numbers do not include the deaths of an estimated half-million defenseless Cambodians and Laotians, on whom the US also dropped a staggering tonnage of bombs. (en.wikipedia.org /wiki/Vietnam_war) An unknown number of Vietnamese have suffered spontaneous abortion, stillbirth, cancer, and other devasting effects since the war from the 20 million gallons of dioxin-containing defoliants such as Agent Orange the United States sprayed over 10% of the country (42% on food crops, the remainder on the jungle forests) (en.wikipedia.org /wiki/Agent_Orange). A

recent study by a Canadian team found levels of contamination around Da
Nang, a typical city, at 300–400 times the level considered minimally safe, 30
years after the end of the conflict
(www.terrapub.co.jp/onlineproceedings/ec/02/pdf/ERA3.pdf), and Vietnam
says that 3 million people have been affected. The birth-defect rate in Vietnam
is many times that in other countries, yielding a horrific legacy in human
suffering (www.chicagotribune.com /health/agentorange/,
http://www.agentorangerecord.com /impact_on_vietnam/health/disabilities1/).
In Iraq, U.S.-led sanctions and the deliberate targeting of Iraq's water and
electrical systems led directly to "half a million. . .deaths of children
under-five" during the Clinton administration (UNICEF, 12 August 1999), a
fact admitted to by the then U.S. Secretary of State, Madeline Albright, who
opined in an interview with journalist Leslie Stahl (CBS, 60-Minutes, 5/12/96)
that the human cost was "worth it." That country is also now widely
contaminated by carcinogenic and birth-defect-causing depleted uranium dust,
ensuring that the civilian death rate will be much higher than normal for
decades to come (www.wsws.org /articles/2005/may2005/iraq-m10.shtml).
These deaths will be in addition to the hundreds of thousands of civilians killed
outright in the invasion and occupation of Iraq (en.wikipedia.org
/wiki/Casualties_of_the_Iraq_War). These are just the principle, most direct,
and least controversial episodes of mass civilian death at the hands of the
United States in the last several decades. As the world's foremost weapons
supplier and military hegemon, it is indirectly responsible for many more of
the past half-century's massacres, even when it was not directly involved.

[25] A study in October 2003 by the Program on International Policy Attitudes
(PIPA) found that those Americans who watched cable or commercial network
news were more likely to have significant misperceptions about Iraqi WMD's,
about Iraq's involvement in the 9-11 attacks, and about attitudes in other
countries towards the American invasion of Iraq (65.109.167.118
/pipa/pdf/oct03/IraqMedia_Oct03_rpt.pdf). More recent studies have confirmed
that corporate owned public information sources would be more aptly named
"public misinformation sources." (www.worldpublicopinion.org
/pipa/pdf/dec10/Misinformation_Dec10_rpt.pdf)

[26] Actually, these figures are out of date because they were calculated before
the 2008 collapse that devastated household net worth for most Americans.
The imbalance has increased dramatically since then. (en.wikipedia.org
/wiki/Distribution_of_wealth#In_the_United_States)

[27] Federal minimum sentences for drug trafficking range variously from 5 years
to life in prison, depending on the type and amount of substance involved and
prior convictions. For an analysis by the United States Sentencing Commission

in 1991, see http://www.ussc.gov /r_congress/MANMIN.PDF.

[28]For-profit detention centers sprang up in the 1980's and flourished. As of 2012, about 8% of all prisoners were incarcerated in privately run facilities, and more than 10% of federal prisoners, acccording to propublica.org . The largest, Corrections Corporation of America, had revenues of $1.7 billion in 2011, and it boasts that it is the nation's 5th largest prison system—behind only the federal government and three states—with facilities in almost half the states. (www.cca.com /about)

[29]There are currently more than 2.2 million inmates in federal, state, and local prisons and jails, more than 700 per 100,000 population. (www.sentencingproject.org /template/page.cfm?id=107) Roughly half of these are for non-violent offenses, primarily drug and property offenses (www.ojp.usdoj.gov /bjs/prisons.htm). The number of prisoners worldwide is slightly more than 9 million (www.csdp.org /research/r234.pdf). Using US and world population figures from the CIA world fact book (www.cia.gov /cia/publications/factbook/), it can be calculated that the US, with less than 5% of the world's population, holds nearly 25% of its prisoners.

[30]Many of these 500,000 mentally ill prisoners are in prisons at least in part because there are no mental health facilities to take them. Most are severely mentally ill, suffering from schizophrenia, bipolar disorder, or other psychoses (www.pbs.org /wgbh/pages/frontline/shows/asylums/).

[31]"The U.S. is the only United Nations member-state except Somalia that has neglected to ratify the UN's 1989 Convention on the Rights of the Child. In February 2001, George W. Bush explicitly objected to its 'human rights-based approach' which, among other things, prohibits prosecuting and incarcerating children as adults because their minds are too immature to form 'criminal intent.' Indeed, the U.S. stands alone in its rush to sentence children to a lifetime in prison without the possibility of parole, and is home to more than 99 percent of youths serving this sentence worldwide. According to a joint 2005 study by Human Rights Watch and Amnesty International, the U.S. had 9,400 prisoners serving life prison terms for crimes committed before the age of 18, of which 2,225 were serving life without parole. Of those, 16% were between 13 and 15 years old at the time they committed the crimes for which they were convicted. More than 100,000 children are currently incarcerated in local detention and state correctional institutions across the country." Sharon Smith, writing in CounterPunch (www.counterpunch.org /sharon04252007.html).

[32]*National Defense Authorization Act for Fiscal Year 2012.* Wikipedia. (en.wikipedia.org /wiki/National_Defense_Authorization_Act_for_Fiscal_Year_2012)

[33]Jo Becker and Scott Shane. *Secret Kill List Proves a Test of Obama's Principles and Will.* The New York Times. (www.nytimes.com /2012/05/29/world/obamas-leadership-in-war-on-al-qaeda.html?_r=1)

[34]An excellent summary of the United States' human rights record is provided by Amnesty International at http://www.amnesty.org /en/region/usa.

[35]A BBC World Service poll of 26,000 people in 25 countries (released 1/23/2007) showed broad disapproval of US behavior, with roughly 2/3 expressing disapproval of such aspects of US foreign policy as the invasion of Iraq, relations with Iran, Mideast peace generally, the "war on terror", and global warming (www.globescan.com /news_archives/bbcusop). Sixty-eight percent agreed with the statement that US foreign policy causes more conflict than it prevents. A Pew Global Attitudes Project Poll found majority disapproval of the US in 10 out of 14 countries polled. An analysis of these polls show that while people around the world reject US policies, they continue to embrace its values (www.worldpublicopinion.org /pipa/articles/views_on_countriesregions_bt/326.php).

[36]A Pew Research poll in 2006 found a majority in most countries viewed the United States' presence in Iraq as the greatest threat to world peace (pewglobal.org /reports/display.php?ReportID=252). A poll conducted by The Guardian in Britain, Haaretz in Israel, Reforma in Mexico, and the Toronto Star in Canada found significant majorities identifying U.S. foreign policy as making the world less safe (www.msnbc.msn.com /id/15544601/), with 75% of Britons agreeing with the statement that the U.S. leader is a threat to world peace. Just prior to the invasion of Iraq in 2003, an informal Time poll of European online respondents found that when offered the three choices of Iraq, North Korea, or the United States, a whopping 87% said the U.S. was the greatest threat to peace (www.time.com /time/europe/gdml/peace2003.html). Subsequent polling through 2012 by the Pew Research Center confirms that the United States' image globally has continued to decline under the Obama administration. (www.pewglobal.org)

[37]Edward Bernays. *Propaganda.* 1928. (archive.org /details/EdwardLBernays-Propaganda)

[38]*Committee on Public Information.* Wikipedia. (en.wikipedia.org /wiki/Committee_on_Public_Information)

[39]*Edward Bernays.* Wikipedia. (en.wikipedia.org /wiki/Edward_Bernays)

[40]*Edward Bernays.* Wikipedia. (en.wikipedia.org /wiki/Edward_Bernays#Recognition_and_criticism)

[41]*1954 Guatemalan coup d'état.* Wikipedia. (en.wikipedia.org

/wiki/Operation_PBSUCCESS)

[42]*History of Public Relations.* Wikipedia. (en.wikipedia.org /wiki/History_of_public_relations)

[43]*Bonus Army.* Wikipedia. (en.wikipedia.org /wiki/Bonus_Army)

[44]*Conscription in the United States.* Wikipedia. (en.wikipedia.org /wiki/Conscription_in_the_United_States#World_War_II)

[45]*American Social Policy During the Second Red Scare.* Wikipedia. (en.wikipedia.org /wiki/American_social_policy_during_the_Second_Red_Scare)

[46]*Mission Creep.* Mother Jones. (www.motherjones.com /military-maps)

[47]Victor Lebow. *Price Competition in 1955.* Journal of Retailing. 1955. (hundredgoals.files.wordpress.com /2009/05/journal-of-retailing.pdf)

[48]George Welling. *An Outline of American History.* University of Groningen.(www.let.rug.nl/usa/H/1963/ch4_p3.htm)

[49]Kathy Paulson. *Great Depression Taught Thrift, Conservation.* NRHEG Star Eagle. (www.newrichlandstar.com /jnews/columns/46-whatever/199-great-depression-taught-thrift-conservation.html)

[50]*A Consumer Economy.* U.S. History. (www.ushistory.org /us/46f.asp)

[51]*[The]United States in the 1950s; Capitalism and Consumerism.* Wikipedia. (en.wikipedia.org /wiki/United_States_in_the_1950s#Capitalism_and_consumerism)

[52]*Television.* Wikipedia. (en.wikipedia.org /wiki/Television)

[53]*The Nielsen A2/M2 Three Screen Report.* The Nielsen Company. (blog.nielsen.com /nielsenwire/online_mobile/tv-internet-and-mobile-usage-in-us-continues-to-rise/)

[54]*Boxed In.* The Economist. (www.economist.com /node/14252309?story_id=14252309)

[55]*Average Hour-Long TV Show is 36% Commercials.* Marketing Charts. (www.marketingcharts.com /television/average-hour-long-show-is-36-commercials-9002/)

[56]The average cost of producing a 30-second advertisement is more than $300,000 (www.aaaa.org /news/bulletins/pages/08tvprodcostssur_121109.aspx), and about 20 minutes worth are shown every hour. By contrast, a typical 1-hour episode of a prime-time drama costs between 2 and 3 million dollars, costs typically

recouped through fees charged to advertisers for displaying their ads. (en.wikipedia.org /wiki/Television_program#Budgets_and_revenues)

[57] *Stuffing Our Kids: Should Psychologists Help Advertisers Manipulate Children?* Campaign for a Commercial-Free Childhood.(www.commercialfreechildhood.org /articles/featured/stuffingourkids.htm)

[58] *Advertising as Science.* American Psychological Association. (www.apa.org /monitor/oct02/advertising.aspx)

[59] Margarita Tartakovsky. *The Psychology of Advertising.* World of Psychology. (psychcentral.com /blog/archives/2011/02/15/the-psychology-of-advertising/)

[60] *Industry Facts and Figures.* Public Relations Society of America. (media.prsa.org /prsa+overview/industry+facts+figures/)

[61] *U.S. Online Advertising Spending to Surpass Print in 2012.* eMarketer Press Release. 19 January 2012. (www.emarketer.com /PressRelease.aspx?R=1008788)

[62] *Media Cross-Ownership in the United States.* Wikipedia. (en.wikipedia.org /wiki/Media_cross-ownership_in_the_United_States#The_.22Big_Six.22)

[63] *Interlocking Directorates.* Fairness & Accuracy In Reporting. (www.fair.org /index.php?page=2870)

[64] *Project Censored* is a non-profit media watchdog groups that publishes and annual report of the top censored (i.e., omitted) news stories of the previous year. Overwhelmingly the stories that are censored are those that would be embarrassing to or counter to the agendas of elite corporate and government interests.

[65] *Inside Bohemian Grove.* Fairness and Accuracy In Reporting. (www.fair.org /index.php?page=1489)

[66] Diana Saluri Russo. *Is the Foreign News Bureau Part of the Past?* Global Journalist (www.globaljournalist.org /stories/2010/01/30/is-the-foreign-news-bureau-part-of-the-past/)

[67] Lucinda Fleeson. *Bureau of Missing Bureaus.* American Journalism Review. (www.ajr.org /article.asp?id=3409)

[68] Pamela Constable. *Demise of the Foreign Correspondent.* The Washington Post. (www.washingtonpost.com /wp-dyn/content/article/2007/02/16/AR2007021601713.html)

[69] Matt Nisbet. *That's Infotainment!* Skeptical Inquirer. 30 April 2001.

(www.csicop.org /specialarticles/show/thats_infotainment/)

[70]Mathew Robinson. *Media Coverage of Crime and Criminal Justice.* Carolina Academic Press, 2011. (www.pscj.appstate.edu /media/introduction.html)

[71]Chris Hedges. *Days of Destruction, Days of Revolt.* Nation Books, 2012. (A good interview of Hedges by Bill Moyers is at billmoyers.com /episode/full-show-capitalism%E2%80%99s-%E2%80%98sacrifice-zones%E2%80%99/)

[72]*Amplifying Officials, Squelching Dissent.* Fairness and Accuracy In Reporting. (www.fair.org /index.php?page=1145)

[73]Glenn Greenwald. *How the U.S. Government Uses Its Media Servants to Attack Real Journalsim.* Salon.com (www.salon.com /2011/07/15/somalia_3/)

[74]Glenn Greenwald. *How the Obama Adminstration is Making the uS Media Its Mouthpiece.* The Guardian. 8 June 2012. (www.guardian.co.uk/commentisfree/2012/jun/08/obama-administration-making-us-media-its-mouthpiece)

[75]Giles Slade. *Made to Break: Technology and Obsolescence in America.* Harvard UP, 2006.

[76]Hannah Fairfield. *Factory Food.* The New York Times. (www.nytimes.com /2010/04/04/business/04metrics.html)

[77]*Is College Worth It?* Pew Research Center. (www.pewsocialtrends.org /2011/05/15/is-college-worth-it/)

[78]In his speech after being named Romney's vice presidential running mate, Rep. Paul Ryan was "echoing Bill Clinton by promising to reward people who 'work hard and play by the rules.' " Howard Kurtz. The Daily Beast. 11 Aug 2012. (www.thedailybeast.com /articles/2012/08/11/mitt-romney-with-nod-to-right-wing-rolls-out-paul-ryan-as-his-running-mate.html)

[79]Vincent Fernando. *This Manufacturer Can't Find 100 Unemployed Americans with Basic Math Skills.* Business Insider. (articles.businessinsider.com /2010-07-02/markets/30017834_1_job-applications-math-unemployment)

[80]Elliot A Medrich and Geanne E. Griffith. *International Mathematics and Science Assessment: What Have We Learned?* National Center for Education Statistics, U.S. Department of Education. (0-nces.ed.gov.opac.acc.msmc.edu /pubs92/92011.pdf)

[81]Sam Dillon. *In Test, Few Students Are Proficient Writers.* The New York Times. (www.nytimes.com /2008/04/03/education/03cnd-writing.html)

[82]*Arts Education in America.* National Endowment for the Arts.
(www.nea.gov/research/2008-SPPA-ArtsLearning.pdf)

[83]Melanie Smolin. *Putlic Education's Dying Arts.* Take Part.
(www.takepart.com /article/2009/06/16/public-educations-dying-arts)

[84]*Literary Reading in Dramatic Decline...* National Endowment for the Arts.
(www.nea.gov/news/news04/readingatrisk.html)

[85]William M. Chace. *The Decline of the English Department.* The American
Scholar. (theamericanscholar.org /the-decline-of-the-english-department/)

[86]*Our Fading Heritage.* Intercollegiate Studies Institute.
(www.americancivicliteracy.org /2008/summary_summary.html)

[87]*America's Civic Learning Crisis.* Campaign for the Civic Mission of
Schools. (www.cms-ca.org /CivicsFactSheet2011.pdf)

[88]*The American-Western European Values Gap.* Pew Research Center.
(www.pewglobal.org
/2011/11/17/the-american-western-european-values-gap/)

[89]Timothy Noah. *The United States of Inequality.* Slate. 3 September 2010.
(www.slate.com
/articles/news_and_politics/the_great_divergence/features/2010/
the_united_states_of_inequality/introducing_the_great_divergence.html)

[90]Darryl William. *America's Rank Drops in Life Expectancy, Education, and
Health Care.* Indy Bay. (www.indybay.org
/newsitems/2012/07/03/18716887.php)

[91]American voter turnout is the lowest in the world. See for instance the
Wikipedia entry at (en.wikipedia.org /wiki/Voter_turnout)

[92]Edward S. Herman and Noam Chomsky. *Manufacturing Consent: The
political Economy of the Mass Media.* Random House, 1988.

[93]Benjamin Schwarz. *American Inequality: Its History and Scary Future.* The
New York Times. 19 December 1995. (www.afn.org
/d̃ks/income/inequality-schwarz.html)

[94]Benjamin Schwarz. *American Inequality: Its History and Scary Future.* The
New York Times. 19 December 1995. (www.afn.org
/d̃ks/income/inequality-schwarz.html)

[95]*Distribution of Family Income—Gini Index.* CIA World Factbook.
(www.cia.gov/library/publications/the-world-factbook/fields/2172.html)

[96]*Income, Poverty, and Health Insurance Coverage in the united States: 2010.*

United States Census Bureau. September 2011.
(www.census.gov/prod/2011pubs/p60-239.pdf)

[97]Timothy Noah. *The United States of Inequality.* Slate. 3 September 2010.
(www.slate.com /articles/news_and_politics/the_great_divergence/features/2010
/the_united_states_of_inequality /introducing_the_great_divergence.html)

[98]*Michael Moore says 400 Americans have more wealth than half of all
Americans combined.* Politifact. 10 March 2011. (www.politifact.com
/wisconsin/statements/2011/mar/10/michael-moore/michael-moore-says-400-
americans-have-more-wealth-/)

[99]G. William Domhoff. *Who Rules America?* University of California, Santa
Cruz. (www2.ucsc.edu /whorulesamerica/power/wealth.html)

[100]*Executive PayWatch.* AFL-CIO. (www.aflcio.org
/Corporate-Watch/CEO-Pay-and-the-99)

[101]Daniel Costello. *The Drought Is Over (at Least for C.E.O.'s)* The New York
Times. 9 April 2011. (www.nytimes.com
/2011/04/10/business/10comp.html?_r=1)

[102]*Total Unemployed (U6Rate).* Federal Reserve Bank of St. Louis. 3 August
2012. (research.stlouisfed.org /fred2/series/U6RATE)

[103]John Williams. *Alternate Unemployment Charts.* Shadow Government
Statistics. (www.shadowstats.com /alternate_data/unemployment-charts)

[104]Rex Nutting. *How the Bubble Destroyed the Middle Class.* The Wall Street
Journal. 8 July 2011. (articles.marketwatch.com
/2011-07-08/commentary/30711408_1_middle-class-wealth-housing-bubble)

[105]*Planning to Retire* U.S. News and World Report. 13 March 2009.
(money.usnews.com /money/blogs/planning-to-retire/2009/03/13/retirement-
accounts-have-now-lost-34-trillion)

[106]Elizabeth Mendes. *In U.S., Fear of Big Government at Near-Record Level.*
Gallup. 12 December 2011. (www.gallup.com
/poll/151490/fear-big-government-near-record-level.aspx)

[107]*Big Donors Swamp Small Donors.* electoral-vote.com.
(www.electoral-vote.com /evp2012/Pres/Maps/Aug03.html#item-2)

[108]R. Jeffrey Smith and Dan Eggen. *Lobbyists Flock to Capitol Hill Jobs.* The
Washington Post. 17 March 2011. (www.washingtonpost.com
/politics/lobbyists-flock-to-capitol-hill-jobs/2011/03/04/ABh7eAn_story.html)

[109]Steve Benen. *Lobbyists Go Back to Writing Laws.* Washington Monthly. 18

March 2011. (www.washingtonmonthly.com
/archives/individual/2011_03/028512.php)

[110]Anna Palmer. *House Republicans Huddle with Lobbyists to Kill Financial Reform Bill.* Roll Call. 8 December 2009. (www.rollcall.com
/news/-41311-1.html)

[111]Derek Thompson. *Google's CEO: The Laws Are Written by Lobbyists.* The Atlantic. 1 October 2010. (www.theatlantic.com
/technology/archive/2010/10/googles-ceo-the-laws-are-written-by-lobbyists/63908/)

[112]*ALEC: The Voice of Corporate Special Interests In State Legislatures.* People for the American Way. (www.pfaw.org
/rww-in-focus/alec-the-voice-of-corporate-special-interests-state-legislatures)

[113]James B. Stewart. *In Superrich, Clues to What Might Be in Romney's Returns.* The New York Times. 10 August 2012. (www.nytimes.com
/2012/08/11/business/in-the-superrich-clues-to-romneys-tax-returns-common-sense.html?_r=2)

[114]Sam Pizzigati. *Mitt's Offshore Shenanigans: The Bigger Story.* Too Much. 21 July 2012. (toomuchonline.org /mitts-offshore-shenanigans-tax-havens/)

[115]*Estimating the Price of Offshore.* Tax Justice Network. 22 July 2012. (www.taxjustice.net/cms/front_content.php?idcat=148)

[116]Bernard Condon. *Study: Companies paid more to CEOs than in US Tax.* Associated Press. 16 August 2012. (hosted.ap.org
/dynamic/stories/U/US_CEO_PAY_TAXES
?SITE=VARIT&SECTION=HOME&TEMPLATE=DEFAULT&CTIME=2012-08-16-10-17-27)

[117]Barry Ritholtz. *Corporate Tax Rates, Then and Now.* The Big Picture. 14 April 2011. (www.ritholtz.com
/blog/2011/04/corporate-tax-rates-then-and-now/)

[118]*The Corporate Welfare State.* The Wall Street Journal. 8 November 2011. (online.wsj.com
/article/SB10001424052970204002304576631192120542046.html)

[119]*Government Spends More on Corporate Welfare Subsidies than Social Welfare Programs.* Think By Numbers. (thinkbynumbers.org
/government-spending/corporate-welfare/corporate-welfare-statistics-vs-social-welfare-statistics/)

[120]*Savings and Loan Crisis.* Wikipedia. (en.wikipedia.org

/wiki/Savings_and_loan_crisis#Consequences)

[121]*Fannie, Freddie Could Cost Taxpayers $169 Billion Through 2012.* Huffington Post. 14 February 2011. (www.huffingtonpost.com /2011/02/14/fannie-freddie-could-cost_n_823173.html)

[122]*Treasury Raises TARP Cost Estimate as Share Prices Shift.* Fox Business. 13 August 2012. (www.foxbusiness.com /news/2012/08/13/treasury-raises-tarp-cost-estimate-as-share-prices-shift/)

[123]Shahien Nasiripour. *Largest Banks Likely Profited By Borrowing From Federal Reserve, Lending to Federal Government.* Huffington Post. 26 April 2011. (www.huffingtonpost.com /2011/04/26/fed-lending-helped-wall-street_n_853884.html)

[124]Mark Pittman and Bob Ivry. *Financial Rescue Nears GDP as Pledges Top $12.8 Trillion.* Bloomberg. 31 March 2009. (www.bloomberg.com /apps/news?pid=newsarchive&sid=armOzfkwtCA4)

[125]*Stewart claims that the stimulus bill is one-third tax cuts.* Politifact.com 10 February 2010. (www.politifact.com /truth-o-meter/statements/2010/feb/10/jon-stewart/stewart-claims-stimulus-bill-one-third-tax-cuts/)

[126]*General Mining Act of 1872.* Wikipedia. (en.wikipedia.org /wiki/General_Mining_Act_of_1872#)

[127]Karyn Moskowitz and Chuck Romaniello. *Assessing the Full Cost of the Federal Grazing Program.* Center for Biological Diversity. October 2002. (www.publiclandsranching.org /htmlres/pdf/Assessing_the_Full_Cost.pdf)

[128]*Your Master's Voice.* Wired. (www.wired.com /wired/archive/5.08/netizen_pr.html)

[129]Lori Montgomery. *Special Interests Win in Senate Panel's Attempt at Tax Reform.* Washington Post. 2 August 2012. (www.washingtonpost.com /business/economy/special-interests-win-in-senate-panels-attempt-at-tax-reform/2012/08/02/gJQASwL1SX_story.html)

[130]*The Military Industrial Complex.* Wikipedia. (en.wikipedia.org /wiki/Military%E2%80%93industrial_complex)

[131]*United States Federal Budget.* Wikipedia. (en.wikipedia.org /wiki/United_States_federal_budget)

[132]Budget of the United States Government, Fiscal Year 2012, Historical Table 3.1. (www.whitehouse.gov/sites/default/files/omb/budget/fy2012/assets/hist.pdf)

[133]*Where Your Income Tax Money Really Goes.* War Resisters League. (www.warresisters.org /pages/piechart.htm)

[134]*The US Defense Industry and Arms Sales.* Stanford University. (www.stanford.edu /class/e297a/U.S. Defense Industry and Arms Sales.htm)

[135]*Military Budget.* Wikipedia. (en.wikipedia.org /wiki/Military_budget)

[136]Costs of War. (costsofwar.org)

[137]*The US Defense Industry and Arms Sales.* Stanford University. (www.stanford.edu /class/e297a/U.S. Defense Industry and Arms Sales.htm)

[138]*Defense Contractor.* Wikipedia. (en.wikipedia.org /wiki/Defense_contractor)

[139]*Interest Groups.* Center for Responsive Politics. (www.opensecrets.org /industries/index.php)

[140]*The 25 Most Vicious Iraq War Profiteers.* Business Pundit. (www.businesspundit.com /the-25-most-vicious-iraq-war-profiteers/)

[141]Great Books Online. (www.bartleby.com /73/991.html)

[142]Glenn Greenwald. *With Liberty and Justice for Some.* Macmillan: Picador. July 2012.

[143]For the mathematically inclined: A pinch is 1/16 of a teaspoon, there are 6 teaspoons in an ounce, and 128 ounces in a gallon. So there are 12,288 pinches in a gallon. Taking the logarithm to base 2 shows that the fungus doubles about 13.6 times to fill the jug, or once every 7 hours or so over the course of 96 hours.

[144]*World Population.* Wikipedia. (en.wikipedia.org /wiki/World_population#Overpopulation)

[145]This figure is based on a current total human population growth rate of 1.1%. See for example Wikipedia, (en.wikipedia.org /wiki/World_population)

[146]Mathis Wackernagel, et al. *Tracking the Ecological Overshoot of the Human Economy.* Proceedings of the National Academy of Sciences of the United States of America. 16 May 2002. (www.pnas.org /content/99/14/9266)

[147]*Earth Overshoot Day.* Global Footprint Network. (www.footprintnetwork.org /en/index.php/GFN/page/earth_overshoot_day/)

[148]*Malthusianism.* Wikipedia. (en.wikipedia.org /wiki/Malthusianism)

[149]*Foresight. The Future of Food and Farming (2011).* Government Office for Science (United Kingdom), London.

(www.bis.gov.uk/assets/foresight/docs/food-and-farming/11-547-future-of-food-and-farming-summary.pdf)

[150]*Green Revolution.* Wikipedia. (en.wikipedia.org /wiki/Green_Revolution)

[151]*Human Appropriation of the World's Food Supply.* University of Michigan. (www.globalchange.umich.edu /globalchange2/current/lectures/food_supply/food.htm)

[152]*Food Security.* Wikipedia. (en.wikipedia.org /wiki/Food_security)

[153]*Food Production Must Double by 2050. . ..* United Nations General Assembly, Report to Second Committee. 9 October 2009. (www.un.org /News/Press/docs/2009/gaef3242.doc.htm)

[154]Sam Williford. *U.S. On Pace to Export Record Amount of Food in 2010–11.* Economy in Crisis. 5 December 2010. (economyincrisis.org /content/us-pace-export-record-amount-food-2010-11)

[155]*Ogallala Aquifer.* Wikipedia. (en.wikipedia.org /wiki/Ogallala_Aquifer)

[156]Amanda Mascarelli. *Demand for Water Outstrips Supply.* Nature. 8 August 2012. (www.nature.com /news/demand-for-water-outstrips-supply-1.11143)

[157]Shirin Wertime. *Energy Use in the US & Global Agri-Food Systems: Implications for Sustainable Agriculture.* Culture Change. 5 June 2010. (www.culturechange.org /cms/content/view/652/1/)

[158]*Peak Oil.* Wikipedia. (en.wikipedia.org /wiki/Peak_oil)

[159]*Crude Oil, Average Spot Price Chart.* Mongabay.com. (www.mongabay.com /images/commodities/charts/crude_oil.html)

[160]*World Must Brace for Higher Food Prices, Experts Warn.* Gulf Times/AFP. 20 August 2012. (www.gulf-times.com /site/topics/article.asp ?cu_no=2&item_no=526141&version=1&template_id=48&parent_id=28)

[161]*2007&ndash2008 World Food Price Crisis.* Wikipedia. en.wikipedia.org /wiki/2007%E2%80%932008_world_food_price_crisis)

[162]Vandana Shiva. *The Green Revolution in the Punjab.* The Ecologist, Vol. 21, No. 2, March April 1991. (livingheritage.org /green-revolution.htm)

[163]*Fertility (soil).* Wikipedia. (en.wikipedia.org /wiki /Fertility_(soil)#Soil_depletion)

[164]Tom Paulson. *The Lowdown on Topsoil: It's Disappearing.* Seattle PI. 21 January 2008. (www.seattlepi.com /national/article/The-lowdown-on-topsoil-It-s-disappearing-1262214.php#page-1)

[165]*Loss of Arable Land.* Sustainable Settlement in Southern Africa. (www.sustainablesettlement.co.za/issues/landloss.html)

[166]*World Food Supply.* United Nations Environment Programme (UNEP). 2011. (www.grida.no/publications/rr/food-crisis/page/3562.aspx)

[167]Evan O'Neil and William Vocke. *Declining Fish Stocks.* Policy Innovations. 10 September 2010. (www.policyinnovations.org /ideas/video/data/000340)

[168]*Big-Fish Stocks Fall 90 Percent Since 1950, Study Says.* National Geographic News. 15 May 2003. (news.nationalgeographic.com /news/2003/05/0515_030515_fishdecline.html)

[169]Mat McDermott. *More Factory Farms Behind 20% Increase in Meat Consumption Over Past Decade.* Trehugger. 12 October 2011. (www.treehugger.com /green-food/more-factory-farms-behind-20-increase-in-meat-consumption-over-past-decade.html)

[170]*Meat Production Continues to Rise.* Worldwatch Institute. (www.worldwatch.org /node/5443)

[171]David Pimentel and marcia Pimentel. *Sustainability of Meat-based and Plant-based diets and the Environment.* The American Journal of Clinical Nutrition, vol. 78 no. 3, September 2003. (www.ajcn.org /content/78/3/660S.full)

[172]*Desertification.* Wikipedia. (en.wikipedia.org /wiki/Desertification)

[173]John Vidal. *Soil Erosion Threatens to Leave Earth Hungry.* The Guardian. 14 December 2010. (www.guardian.co.uk/environment/2010/dec/14/soil-erosion-environment-review-vidal)

[174]*Shrinking Arable land Threatens Grain Security.* China Daily. 18 October 2010. (www.chinadaily.com.cn/china/2010-10/18/content_11423618.htm)

[175]*Scientific Facts on Desertification.* Green Facts. (www.greenfacts.org /en/desertification/l-3/6-prevention-desertification.htm)

[176]*Human Appropriation of the World's Food Supply.* Global Change, University of Michigan. 4 January 2006. (www.globalchange.umich.edu /globalchange2/current/lectures/food_supply/food.htm)

[177]*Land Degradation and Water Shortages Threaten Global Food Production.* UN News Centre. 28 November 2011. (www.un.org /apps/news/story.asp?NewsID=40533)

[178]*Climate Change and Security.* Oxfam Fact Sheet. Spring 2009. (www.oxfamamerica.org /files/climate-change-and-security-fact-sheet.pdf)

[179]*Water Crisis*. Wikipedia. (en.wikipedia.org /wiki/Water_crisis)

[180]C.J. Vorosmarty, et al. *Global Threats to Human Water Security and River Biodiversity*. Nature, no. 467, 30 September 2010. (www.nature.com /nature/journal/v467/n7315/full/nature09440.html)

[181]Alex Kerby. *Dawn of a Thirsty Century*. BBC News. 2 June 2000. (news.bbc.co.uk/2/hi/science/nature/755497.stm)

[182]Richard Mills. *Ecological Overshoot*. Ahead Of The Herd.(aheadoftheherd.com /Newsletter/2011/Ecological-overshoot.html)

[183]*Municipal Solid Waste Generation, Recycling, and Disposal in the United States: Facts and Figures for 2010*. United States Environmental Protection Agency. (www.epa.gov/osw/nonhaz/municipal/pubs/msw_2010_rev_factsheet.pdf)

[184]Veronica Smith. *World's City Dwellers Face Garbage Crisis*. AFP. 6 June 2012. (www.google.com /hostednews/afp/article/ALeqM5jzdoDoNX9susEpDmlK3LNMaasbyw ?docId=CNG.b2b6d9f7ce6adf5bed58011e6ead2cda.e1)

[185]Mutasem El-Fadel, et al. *Environmental Impacts of Solid Waste Landfilling*. Journal of Environmental Management, vol. 50, no. 1. May 1997. (www.sciencedirect.com /science/article/pii/S0301479785701314)

[186]*Plastic Debris in the World's Oceans*. Greenpeace and the United Nations Environment Programme. (www.unep.org /regionalseas/marinelitter/publications/docs/plastic_ocean_report.pdf)

[187]*Marine Debris in the North Pacific: Frequent Questions*. United States Environmental Protection Agency. (www.epa.gov/region9/marine-debris/faq.html)

[188]Lindsey Hoshaw. *Afloat in the Ocean, Expanding Islands of Trash*. New York Times. 9 November 2009. (www.nytimes.com /2009/11/10/science/10patch.html?_r=1&ref=science)

[189]*Water for Life Decade: Water Quality*. United Nations Department of Economic and Social Affairs. (www.un.org /waterforlifedecade/quality.shtml)

[190]*The Mighty Mississippi: Impacts to the River*. Big River Citizens Education Guide. Missouri Department of Natural Resources. (www.dnr.mo.gov /education/bigriver/the mississippi river/impacts to river.pdf)

[191]*How Much Oil Have We Used?* Science Daily. 8 May 2009. (www.sciencedaily.com /releases/2009/05/090507072830.htm)

[192]*Oil Reserves.* Wikipedia. (en.wikipedia.org /wiki/Oil_reserves)

[193]Using the Chevy Volt for comparison, a compact car designed for efficiency, we find that a 13 kilowatt-hour charge will take the Volt about as far, depending on conditions such as ambient air temperature, as 1 gallon of gasoline will take it, according to Chevrolet's published data. (www.chevroletvoltage.com /index.php/volt-blog/18-volt/2595-chevrolet-volt-math-everybody-can-understand.html, en.wikipedia.org /wiki/Electric_car#Running_costs_and_maintenance)

[194]Mark Modica. *Chevy Volt Gas Savings: Myths and Reality.* 27 February 2012. National Legal and Policy Center. (nlpc.org /stories/2012/02/24/true-gas-savings-chevy-volt)

[195]*One Gallon—The Achilles' Heel of Electric Cars.* Red State. 19 February 2012. (www.redstate.com /brookhaven/2012/02/19/one-gallon-%E2%80%93-the-achilles-heel-of-electric-cars/)

[196]A photovoltaic system in southern latitudes may expect to produce 1 Wh/m$\hat{2}$/day (en.wikipedia.org /wiki/Photovoltaic_system) and a 5 kilowatt system would require about 40 square meters of collectors (www.californiasolarco.com /faq.html).

[197]*The Cost of Generating Electricity.* Royal Academy of Engineering. (www.raeng.org.uk /news/publications/list/reports /cost_generation_commentary.pdf)

[198]Michael Grunwald. *The Real Cost of U.S. Nuclear Power.* Time. 25 March 2011. (www.time.com /time/magazine/article/0,9171,2059603,00.html)

[199]Arne Jungjohann. *Germany's Phaseout Reveals the True Costs of Nuclear Power.* 30 September 2011. (grist.org /nuclear/2011-09-29-germanys-phaseout-reveals-the-true-costs-of-nuclear-power/)

[200]Damian Carrington. *Nuclear Power's Real Chain Reaction: Spiralling Costs.* The Guardian.22 July 2011. (www.guardian.co.uk/environment/damian-carrington-blog/2011/jul/22/nuclear-power-cost-delay-edf)

[201]*Food vs. Fuel.* Wikipedia. (en.wikipedia.org /wiki/Food_vs._fuel)

[202]*The Ethanol Fallacy.* Popular Mechanics. 18 December 2009. (www.popularmechanics.com /cars/alternative-fuel/biofuels/4237539)

[203]*Ask the Conservationist: January 2011: Why Does Biodiversity Matter?* The Nature Conservancy. (www.nature.org /ourscience/sciencefeatures/ask-the-conservationist-january-2011.xml)

[204]*What Does Biodiversity Do for Us?* Bio Diversity BC.
(www.biodiversitybc.org /EN/main/why/109.html)

[205]*Millennium Ecosystem Assessment.* (www.maweb.org /en/index.aspx)

[206]*The Sixth Great Extinction?* Biotechnology and Biological Sciences
Research Council. (United Kingdom.)
(www.bbsrc.ac.uk/biodiversity/why/sixth-extinction.html)

[207]Anthony D. Barnosky, et al. *Has the Earth's Sixth Mass Extinction Already
Arrived?* Nature, no. 471. 2 March 2011. (www.nature.com
/nature/journal/v471/n7336/abs/nature09678.html)

[208]*How do Human Activities Contribute to Climate Change and How do They
Compare with Natural Influences?* National Oceanic and Atmospheric
Administration.
(oceanservice.noaa.gov/education/pd/climate/factsheets/howhuman.pdf)

[209]*Causes of Climate Change.* Directgov. (United Kingdom.)
(www.direct.gov.uk /en/Environmentandgreenerliving/Thewiderenvironment
/Climatechange/DG_072920)

[210]*Research Links Extreme Summer Heat Events to Global Warming.* National
Aeronautics and Space Administration.
(www.nasa.gov/topics/earth/features/warming-links.html)

[211]*Human-Caused Climate Change a Major Factor in More Frequent
Mediterranean Droughts.* National Oceanic and Atmospheric Administration.
27 October 2011.
(www.noaanews.noaa.gov/stories2011/20111027_drought.html)

[212]*Stronger Evidence for Human-Induced Climate Change.* Commonwealth
Scientific and industrial Research Organisation. (Australia.)
(www.csiro.au/Organisation-Structure/Divisions/Marine–Atmospheric-
Research/Stronger-evidence-for-human-induced-climate-change.aspx)

[213]*Global Warming & Climate Change.* The New York Times.
(topics.nytimes.com /top/news/science/topics/globalwarming/index.html)

[214]*Effects of Global Warming, Long-term Effects of Global Warming.*
Wikipedia. (en.wikipedia.org /wiki/Effects_of_global_warming,
en.wikipedia.org /wiki/Long-term_effects_of_global_warming)

[215]*The Current and Future Consequences of Global Change.* National
Aeronautics and Space Administration. (climate.nasa.gov/effects/)

[216]*Effects of Global Warming: Abrupt or Irreversible Changes.* Wikipedia.
(en.wikipedia.org /wiki/ Effects_of_global_warming

#Abrupt_or_irreversible_changes)

[217]*Food crises doomed to repeat until leaders find courage to fix problems.* Oxfam Media Advisory. Autust 2012. (www.oxfam.org /sites/www.oxfam.org /files/food-price-crisis-oxfam-media-advisory-aug2012.pdf)

[218]*Earth Overshoot Day.* Footprint Network. (www.footprintnetwork.org /en/index.php/GFN/page/earth_overshoot_day/)

[219]David Pimental and Mario Giampietro. *Food, Land, Population, and the U.S. Economy.* Carrying Capacity Network. 21 November 1994. (www.dieoff.com /page69.htm)

[220]Henry Blodget. *Jeremy Grantham: We're Headed for a Disaster of Biblical Proportions.* Business Insider. 13 June 2011. (www.businessinsider.com /jeremy-grantham-commodity-prices-2011-6?op=1)

[221]*Voter Turnout.* Wikipedia. (en.wikipedia.org /wiki/Voter_turnout)

[222]*What Can Be Done About Long Lines at Polling Places?* Hart Interactive. (www.hartic.com /files/LongLinesWhitePaper.pdf)

[223]*Access to Democracy: Identifying Obstacles Hindering the Right to Vote.* Women's Voices. Women Vote. 15 April 2009. (www.voterparticipation.org /wp-content/uploads/2011/10/WVWV-Access-to-Democracy-Report1.pdf)

[224]*ALEC: The Voice of Corporate Special Interests in State Legislatures.* People for the American Way. (www.pfaw.org /rww-in-focus/alec-the-voice-of-corporate-special-interests-state-legislatures)

[225]*ALEC's Voter ID Laws Work to Overturn Hundreds of Years of Progressive Moves to Broaden Democracy.* Leo Gerard. AlterNet. 7 May 2012. (www.alternet.org /story/155307 /alec's_voter_id_laws_work_to_overturn_hundreds_of_years_of_progressive _moves_to_broaden_democracy)

[226]*Defending Democracy: Confronting Modern Barriers to Voting Rights in America.* Report of the NAACP. (www.naacpldf.org /files/publications/Defending Democracy 12-5-11.pdf)

[227]Greg Allen. *In Florida, Registering Voters a Whole New Game.* National Public Radio. 26 August 2012. (www.npr.org /2012/05/14/152517589/in-florida-registering-voters-a-whole-new-game)

[228]*Voter Suppression: Purging Voter Rolls.* Wikipedia. (en.wikipedia.org /wiki/Voter_suppression#Purging_voter_rolls)

[229]Myrna Pérez. *Voter Purges.* Brennan Center for Justice, New York

University School of Law. 30 September 2008. (www.brennancenter.org /content/resource/voter_purges)

[230]Brendan Fischer. *WI GOP Legislators Call for Voter Purge, Fewer Voter Registrations.* Center for Media and Democracy. 23 July 2012. (www.prwatch.org /news/2012/07/11660/wi-gop-legislators-call-voter-purge-fewer-voter-registrations)

[231]*The Truth About Fraud.* Brennan Center for justice, New York University School of Law. (www.truthaboutfraud.org /)

[232]Amy Goodman. *Obstacles to Voting Return.* The Spokesman-Review. 24 August 2012. *(www.spokesman.com /stories/2012/aug/24/amy-goodman-obstacles-to-voting-return/)

[233]Ari Berman. *The GOP War on Voting.* Rolling Stone. 30 August 2011. (www.rollingstone.com /politics/news/the-gop-war-on-voting-20110830))

[234]*Voters Say Election Full of Misleading and False Information.* World Public Opinion. 9 December 2010. (www.worldpublicopinion.org /pipa/articles/brunitedstatescanadara/671.php)

[235]Kathleen Bawn, et al. *A Theory of Political Parties: Groups, Policy Demands and Nominations in American Politics.* (masket.net/Theory_of_Parties.pdf)

[236]Robert longley. *Half of 18-29 Year-Olds Think Bush Wants to Reinstate Draft.* About.com: US Government Info. (usgovinfo.about.com /od/defenseandsecurity/a/bushdraft.htm)

[237]Benjamin Reeves. *Political Ad Spending For US Presidential Election To Reach $2.9B.* International Business Times. 15 August 2012. (www.emarketer.com /PressRelease.aspx?R=1008788)

[238]Mark Sweney. *Barack Obama campaign claims two top prizes at Cannes Lion ad awards.* The Guardian. 29 June 2009. (www.guardian.co.uk/media/2009/jun/29/barack-obama-cannes-lions)

[239]Matthew Creamer. *Obama Wins! ... Ad Age's Marketer of the Year.* Advertising Age. 17 October 2008. (adage.com /article/moy-2008/obama-wins-ad-age-s-marketer-year/131810/)

[240]*Agenda-setting Theory.* Wikipedia. (en.wikipedia.org /wiki/Agenda-setting_theory)

[241]Arthur Lupia. *Busy Voters, Agenda Control, and the Power of Information.* The American Political Science Review, vol 86, no. 2. (www-personal.umich.edu /~lupia/Papers/Lupia1992_BusyVoters.pdf

[242]Dietram A Acheufele and David Tewksbury. *Framing, Agenda Setting, and Priming: TheEvolution of Three Media Effects Models.* Journal of Communication 57. (www.scienzepolitiche.unimi.it/files/_ITA_/COM/3-Framing-AgendaSetting.pdf)

[243]*Public Priorities: Deficit Rising, Terrrorism Slipping.* Pew Research Center. 23 January 2012. (www.people-press.org /2012/01/23/public-priorities-deficit-rising-terrorism-slipping/)

[244]Ben Baden. *Public Sector Job Cuts Threaten Recovery.* 8 July 2011. (money.usnews.com /money/careers/articles/2011/07/08/public-sector-job-cuts-threaten-recovery)

[245]*Think Government Job Losses Don't Hurt Us? Think Again.* Media Matters for America. 10 June 2012. (mediamatters.org /research/2012/06/10/think-government-job-losses-dont-hurt-us-think/186250)

[246]Mike Conczal and Bryce Covert. *Red States See Massive Public Sector Job Losses.* The Nation. 27 march 2012. (www.thenation.com /article/167050/red-states-see-massive-public-sector-job-losses#)

[247]Michael Cooper. *U.S. Infrastructure Is in Dire Straits, Report Says.* The New York Times. 27 January 2009. (www.nytimes.com /2009/01/28/us/politics/28projects.html)

[248]Jim Naureckas. *Millionaires Working for Billionaires.* Extra!, Sep/Oct 2007. Fairness and Accuracy in Reporting. (www.fair.org /index.php?page=3472)

[249]Chris Wells, et al. *Information Distortion and Voting Choices:The Origins and Effects of Factual Beliefs inInitiative Elections.* Political Psychology, Vol. 30, No. 6, 2009. (www.la1.psu.edu /cas/jgastil/pdfs/InformationDistortion.pdf)

[250]Peter K. Enns, Gregory E. McAvoy. *The Role of Partisanship in Aggregate Opinion.* Political Behavior. Springer Science+Business Media. 14 August 2011. (falcon.arts.cornell.edu /pe52/Enns_McAvoyPartisanshipInAggregateOpinion.pdf)

[251]John G. Bullock. *The Enduring Importance of False Political Beliefs.* Stanford University Dept. of Political Science. 14 March 2006. (citation.allacademic.com /meta/p_mla_apa_research_citation/0/9/7/4/5/ p97459_index.html)

[252]Peter K. Enns and Gregory E. McAvoy. *The Role of Partisanship in the Rational Public.* Cornell University: PERC Seminar. 3 April 2008. (government.arts.cornell.edu /assets/psac/sp08/Enns_McAvoy_April08_PSAC.pdf)

[253]*Why Didn't Obama Change Washington?* Electoral-vote.com 2 September 2012. (www.electoral-vote.com /evp2012/Pres/Maps/Sep02.html#item-1)

[254]Miranda Spenser. *Suppressing the Vote, Suppressing the News.* Fairness and Accuracy in Reporting. January/February 2005. (www.fair.org /index.php?page=2482)

[255]*False Balance Lives At The New York Times.* NYTimes eXaminer. 15 March 2012. (www.nytexaminer.com /2012/03/false-balance-lives-at-the-new-york-times/)

[256]Ryan Chittum. *False balance on Romney's bogus welfare reform attack.* Columbia Journalism Review. 10 August 2012. (www.cjr.org /the_audit/false_equivalence_on_romneys_b_1.php?page=all)

[257]For a stark example of partisan framing, see for instance the Pew Research Center widget for political self-identification at www.people-press.org /political-party-quiz/?result

[258]Chad Rosenbloom. *Congress's Missing Coverage.* Extra! August 2012. Fairness and Accuracy in Reporting. (www.fair.org /index.php?page=4586)

[259]*Spoiler Effect.* Wikipedia. (en.wikipedia.org /wiki/Spoiler_effect)

[260]*Partisan Polarization Surges in Bush, Obama Years.* Pew Research Center. 4 June 2012. (www.people-press.org /2012/06/04/partisan-polarization-surges-in-bush-obama-years/)

[261]*Presidential Ads 70 Percent Negative in 2012, Up from 9 Percent in 2008.* Wesleyan Media Project. 2 May 2012. (mediaproject.wesleyan.edu /2012/05/02/jump-in-negativity/)

[262]Dean Reynolds. *Almost All Presidential Ads on the Air Are Negative.* Kantar Media. 18 July 2012. (kantarmediana.com /cmag/press/almost-all-presidential-ads-air-are-negative?destination=node%2F4%2Fpress)

[263]Robert Jensen. *Saying Goodbye to Patriotism.* CounterPunch. 12 November 2001. (www.counterpunch.org /2001/11/12/goodbye-to-patriotism/)

[264]Glen Martin. *The Corruptions of Patriotism.* (www.counterpunch.org /2003/10/03/the-corruptions-of-patriotism/).

[265]*Terence.* Wikiquote. (en.wikiquote.org /wiki/Terence)

[266]Jackie Calmes. *Obama Marks Fourth With New U.S. Citizens.* The New York Times. 4 July 2012. (www.nytimes.com /2012/07/05/us/politics/obama-starts-fourth-of-july-with-new-citizens.html)

[267]Master Sgt. Jason Haag. *Defenders of Freedom.* Offutt Air Force Base, 55th

Wing Public Affairs. 1 September 2011.
(www.offutt.af.mil/news/story.asp?id=123270490)

[268]Sarah Palin. Vice Presidential Debate, 2008. (www.youtube.com
/watch?v=rjg6mJ28yos)

[269]"America stands alone as the world's indispensable nation." Bill Clinton,
2nd inaugural address, Jan 20th, 1997.

[270]*Fair Labor Standards Act.* Wikipedia. (en.wikipedia.org
/wiki/Fair_Labor_Standards_Act)

[271]*Income Tax in the United States.* Wikipedia. (en.wikipedia.org /wiki/
Income_tax_in_the_United_States#Income_tax_rates_in_history)

[272]*Second Bill of Rights.* Wikipedia. (en.wikipedia.org
/wiki/Second_Bill_of_Rights)

[273]Thomas Jefferson. *A Bill for the More General Diffusion of Knowledge.*
1779. (www.monticello.org
/site/research-and-collections/bill-more-general-diffusion-knowledge)

Index

wildlife, *see* biodiversity, wildlife
World War II
    defense budget higher than at any
        time since, 17
    lessened inequality following, 13
    the good German in, 43

Yellow River, the, 28

ABOUT THE AUTHOR

B. Sidney Smith is a former assistant professor of mathematics and present writer and activist living in central Virginia. He can be reached through his website, bsidneysmith.com.

www.ingramcontent.com/pod-product-compliance
Lightning Source LLC
Chambersburg PA
CBHW070812280326
41934CB00012B/3172